DISCOVER
ORIGAMI

DISCOVER
ORIGAMI

40 ORIGINAL PROJECTS TO BUILD YOUR PAPER CRAFTING SKILLS

RICK BEECH

HAMLYN

First published in Great Britain in 1995 by Hamlyn
an imprint of Reed Consumer Books Limited,
Michelin House, 81 Fulham Road, London SW3 6RB
and Auckland, Melbourne, Singapore and Toronto

TEXT AND PHOTOGRAPHS © 1995
REED INTERNATIONAL BOOKS LIMITED

SERIES PROJECT MANAGER: **MARY LAMBERT**
SERIES PROJECT ART MANAGER: **PRUE BUCKNALL**
ART EDITOR: **ALISON SHACKLETON**
EXECUTIVE EDITOR: **JUDITH MORE**
ART DIRECTOR: **JACQUI SMALL**

PHOTOGRAPHS BY: **LUCY MASON**

The publishers have made every effort to ensure that all instructions
given in this book are accurate and safe, but they cannot accept liability
for any resulting injury, damage or loss to either person or property
whether direct or consequential and howsoever arising. The author and
publishers will be grateful for any information which will assist them in
keeping future editions up to date.

ISBN: 0 600 58593X

DTP ALISON SHACKLETON
PRODUCED BY MANDARIN OFFSET
PRINTED IN HONG KONG

CONTENTS

INTRODUCTION

Origami is a fascinating art form that can become an absorbing hobby. It can be easily taught to children and keep them amused for hours at a party. By simply folding a piece of paper you can transform it into a useful object for your home or into a beautiful piece of art. It is not surprising that origami is one of the most popular crafts as the only material needed – paper – is inexpensive and readily available. No special equipment is normally used and you can fold anywhere – even from an armchair or on a train – providing you work on a firm surface.

You can start off by using some photocopying or inexpensive gift-wrap paper to make models, and when you feel confident in your skills, you can make projects in more expensive papers and give them to people as gifts.

BASIC HISTORY

No one really knows exactly when origami originated, but it didn't exist before paper making was developed by the Chinese around the first century AD. This craft then became part of Japanese culture when Japan was invaded by the Chinese in AD610. Paper was used in Japan to make many practical items, such as screens and mats, but early paper folding models were created for symbolic rather than recreational purposes. In fact, the term for paper folding – origami – is Japanese and is formed from the words "ori" meaning to fold and "kami" meaning paper (and also God).

Origami grew in popularity in the West in Victorian times where it was treated by people as an amusing pastime. But it was not until the 1960s that it became more widely known. A magician called Robert Harbin brought it to the attention of thousands of people, including this book's author, through his television series.

The British Origami Society was formed in 1967 by a group of enthusiasts and there are now societies worldwide. The author Alfred Bestall, who created the character Rupert Bear, was a former president of the society. He was introduced to origami by a Japanese friend and actually included some origami models in his Rupert stories. Origami has also recently undergone a revival in Japan and today there are many books available that are full of different origami creations.

ORIGAMI TODAY

At the present time origami is thriving. Models can be made purely for decoration, but as this book aims to show, origami can also be used to make practical, attractive goods for the home, pretty Christmas ornaments and stunning gifts for friends and relatives.

The skill in origami is in the folding and creasing of the paper. It is not difficult to do, but accuracy is essential to achieve a good-looking model. Many projects in the book are developed from initial bases in the Materials and Techniques section (*see pp. 8–17*). Practise making these bases first so that you can fold them with ease before making the other projects. Details are also given in this section on how to make an accurate square, as most origami creations are developed from a square of paper.

Follow the step-by-step instructions in the projects carefully and note the finished sizes of the model you are making, as the step photographs often show the object in a much smaller size.

Choosing the right type and weight of paper (*see pp. 8–9*) is also important to give the proper finish to a project. Sometimes a lightweight paper is used for a delicate decoration, for example, but on other occasions a heavyweight paper may be chosen for a table item. You also need to take note of the skill levels in the book. If you're a beginner, first tackle the easy models, or you could be frustrated with the more challenging intermediate or advanced ones.

Remember origami is a beautiful, creative craft that should always give pleasure and be thoroughly enjoyed.

MATERIALS AND TECHNIQUES

Origami is not a craft that needs many materials to work with. But before you start making a model, make sure you have a flat surface to fold on, a ruler, pen, a cutting board and a craft knife to trim paper.

PAPER

Photocopying paper is the best type to use for practising origami. Scrap paper, such as torn magazine pages, is also useful.

When you are happy with your practice model, choose the paper for the final version. A good art or craft shop stocks papers with textured or decorative designs, drawing paper, handmade paper, thin watercolour paper and coloured or pastel papers. Packs of one-sided and two-sided coloured squares of origami paper are also available – the 6in (15cm) ones are best for this book's projects.

Gift-wrap paper from stationers is also excellent for folding and comes in many designs and colours. Paper-backed metallic foil is ideal for hanging decorations. Avoid glossy gift-wrap as it does not crease well.

Paper weight is important, so it is listed with the materials. Lightweight paper equals thin airmail paper; mediumweight paper equals drawing paper and any heavyweight paper equals watercolour paper.

In several projects an origami model is placed on a greetings card (see below). Use good-quality cartridge paper for the card, and fix the model in place with paper glue.

HOW TO MAKE A SQUARE

In many of the projects in the book a square piece of paper is needed to make the origami model. Often a standard 6in (15cm) square of origami paper is used, but this paper is quite expensive to buy and you may want to make a square from a more basic paper. Also in other models a larger square needs to be made from gift-wrap paper or other coloured paper.

Always place the paper that you want to cut on a cutting board or a piece of thick card to protect your surface, and to cut away from you with the craft knife. If you use scissors instead, make sure that you cut slowly in a straight line.

Take care when trimming away the excess paper of the square to make the size exact. Your finished model will just not look right if it is made from a square that is not equal on all sides.

1

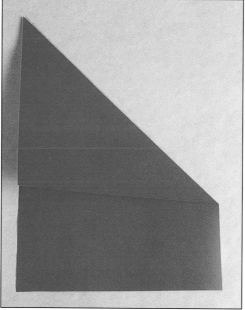

2

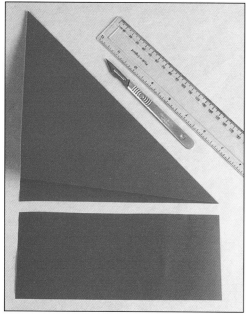

3

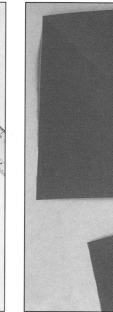

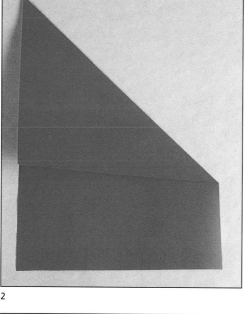

4

MATERIALS

1 sheet of gift-wrap
or coloured paper

Cutting board

Ruler

Craft knife

1 Place the gift-wrap or coloured paper on a cutting board on a firm and even surface.

2 Fold down the top right-hand corner of the paper to the left-hand side to form a triangle with an oblong strip of paper underneath it, as shown.

3 Take the ruler and lay it along the bottom edge of the triangle. Press down and with the craft knife carefully cut off the oblong strip along this line.

4 Open out the triangle to get a perfect square, and then discard the remaining oblong strip.

TIPS

● The square can also be cut with a large pair of scissors.

● You can also cut the square with a kitchen knife, but it takes practice. Fold up the oblong strip and crease well. Then put a sharp knife inside the fold and slice downward, cutting the paper.

HOW TO FOLD

To become proficient at origami, you need to know how to fold paper neatly and evenly. Always do your basic folding on a hard, dry surface, such as a table, keeping the paper flat against it. Sometimes, if a model becomes three-dimensional, for example, you will need to lift it up and work on it above the surface.

The steps in Basic Folding show you how to fold paper in half, bringing points together. This technique is also applied when you fold a square in half with a Book Fold (*see p. 12*), or fold paper behind or in front to make Mountain and Valley Folds (*see p. 12*). Always fold the paper away from the body, as this makes it easier to fold sharp creases. The folding procedure for most models in the book is worked out so that you can achieve this folding direction, while being able to progress naturally to the next step. Always try to align corners and edges accurately as shown in the Blintz Fold (*see p. 12*), where the four points are folded into the middle. In the Squash Fold (*see p. 13*), where a pocket is formed and then squashed flat, you need to hold the model firmly to get the right fold. Origami is a logical art, where most folds are made using certain angles to set locations.

As you fold, look ahead to the next few steps so that you can follow the crease pattern and see how the model is created.

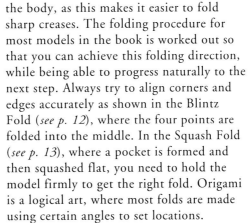

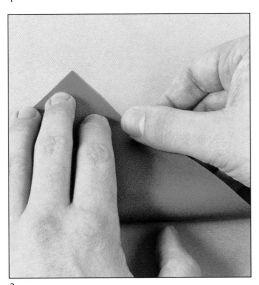

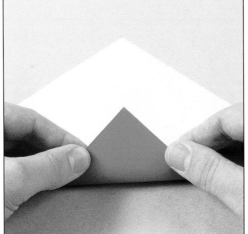

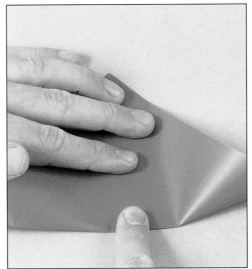

1

2

3

4

TIP

● Practise folding each model on scrap paper first until you feel confident enough to make it with your chosen paper.

BASIC FOLDING

MATERIALS
(for all folding techniques)
1 6in (15cm) square
(or as specified) from a sheet
of coloured paper

1 Start with a square of paper, white side facing upward, in a diamond shape.

2 Take hold of the point nearest you and take it away from the body across to the opposite point.

3 Make sure the two corners touch and that the outer edges align perfectly. Then start to flatten the paper, making a crease horizontally across the paper.

4 Holding the upper portion of the paper to the work surface with one hand, smooth down the crease with the other. You may wish to press the crease very hard by going over it a second time, carefully rubbing it with your thumbnail. Occasionally, a light crease is necessary, where you press very softly on the paper. This is usually when you need to make an initial crease as a guide to a fold that occurs later.

MOUNTAIN AND VALLEY FOLDS

1 To make a mountain fold, first take the square of paper, lay it flat to the work surface, coloured side facing upward in a diamond shape. Then, lifting the paper off the surface, fold the upper point behind, out of sight.

2 To make a valley fold, hold the paper flat to the work surface, lift the bottom point of the paper up and fold in front of the paper, creasing well.

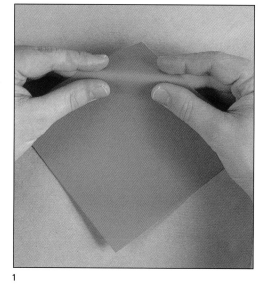

1

2

BOOK FOLD

1 For this book fold, take the square of paper, white side facing upward, and fold in an outside edge to align with a parallel crease line, as shown.

2 The common book fold is to take a square sheet of paper, white side facing upward, and then fold it in half, taking the bottom edge up to the top as shown, or from side to side.

1

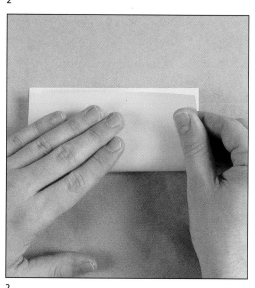

2

BLINTZ FOLD

1 To create a blintz fold, start with the square of paper, white side facing upward, in a diamond shape. Then fold the bottom point up to the top point. Unfold. Then fold from side to side to meet the middle intersecting lines. Unfold.

2 Now carefully fold in the four points of the diamond so that they meet neatly in the middle.

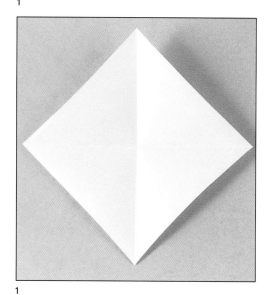

1

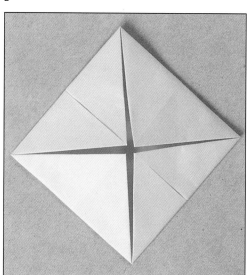

2

SQUASH FOLD

1 Start with the square of paper, white side facing upward, in a diamond shape. Fold in half, taking the bottom point up to the top point.

2 Turn the paper around so that the first crease is vertical, then fold in half again, bringing the bottom point up to the top point.

3 Turn the model around so that the second crease is now vertical. Raise the upper flap until it stands at 90° (right angles) to the flap underneath. Separate the two layers of the flap, pulling slightly apart to give you an opening or pocket.

4 Holding the bottom part of the paper in position, and hollowing out the bottom of the pocket formed in Step 3 with one hand, use your other hand to squash the upper layer down flat. The paper then spreads out to become a diamond.

5 A different type of squash fold can be made on the flaps of the diamond-shaped flap from Step 4. Raise the right-hand flap of this diamond section up to 90° to the rest of the model, separating out the two layers.

6 Hollow out the pocket and squash flat as detailed in steps 1–4. This time, however, a kite shape is formed when the paper is flattened out.

TIP

● Hold model firmly in place when making a squash fold, so that the layers of paper at the base do not splay apart and flatten inaccurately.

1

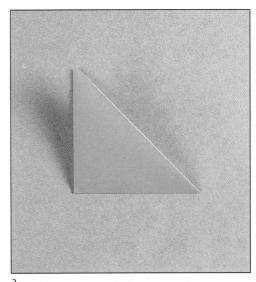

2

3

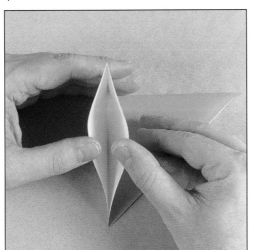

4

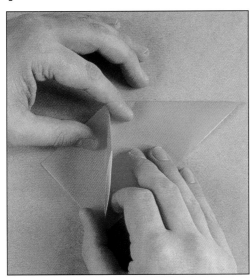

5

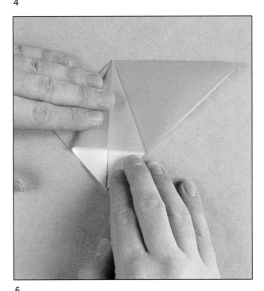

6

HOW TO USE BASES

As origami has developed, several standard bases have evolved with simple folds that act as the starting point for various models. The Preliminary Base, used in projects such as the Party Sailboat (*see p. 24*), involves making four folds in a square which are then collapsed into a diamond shape. The Fish Base, which starts off the three fish in the Fish Mobile (*see pp. 90–93*), opens out into two pockets that are squash folded into the middle. The Waterbomb Base helps to make the Angel (*see pp. 64–65*). It has three folds that flatten right down to make two triangular layers.

PRELIMINARY BASE

MATERIALS

1 6in (15cm) square
(or as specified) from a sheet
of coloured paper

1 Start with the square of paper, coloured side facing upward, in a diamond shape. Then fold the bottom point of the paper up to meet the top point. Unfold.

2 Turn the paper around so that the crease is now vertical, and again fold the bottom point up to meet the top to make the second crease line. Unfold.

3 Turn paper over and arrange it as a square. Put in the first book fold (*see p. 12*) by taking the bottom edge up to meet the top edge. Unfold.

4 Turn the paper around, as in Step 2, so that the crease is now vertical. Fold in half again, taking the bottom edge up to meet the top edge, but this time leave in place.

5 Take hold of the model between your fingers and thumbs, with the folded edge toward you and a little way from the vertical middle crease. Bring all the four corners of the original square together at the top by pushing the sides in toward the middle, so that your fingers and thumbs meet.

6 You now have four flaps in the model, one at the left, one at the right, one in the front and one behind. Using the vertical middle crease as an axis, press the flap pointing toward you across to the right-hand side, so that it lies on top of the existing right flap, as shown. Turn over and repeat the action behind.

1

2

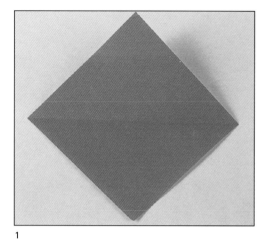

3

4

5

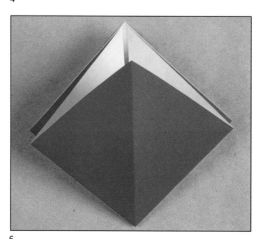

6

FISH BASE

MATERIALS

16in (15cm) square
(or as specified) from a sheet
of coloured paper

1 Start with the square of paper, white side facing upward, in a diamond shape. Fold the right side over to meet the left to establish a vertical middle line. Unfold. Fold the lower right sloping edge inward to align with this middle line.

2 Repeat this fold on the lower left sloping edge.

3 Turn the paper over, keeping the sharp point nearest to you. Fold this point up to touch the top point and crease well into position.

4 Turn the paper back over, keeping it the same way up and flat to the table.

5 Place your fingers inside one of the coloured pockets at the lower part of the model, while holding the other side down flat to the table. Pull the corner of this coloured flap toward you, while at the same time pushing the outer edges of the pocket in toward the vertical middle line. Squash down all the edges and points lining up as shown in the next step.

6 Place your fingers inside the other pocket and repeat Step 5 lining up the edges as shown.

TIP

● Fold the right and sloping edges carefully so that they neatly sit on the middle line, otherwise you will make an inaccurate base.

1

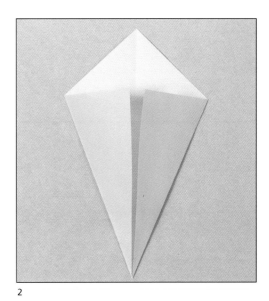

2

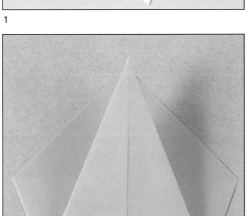

3

4

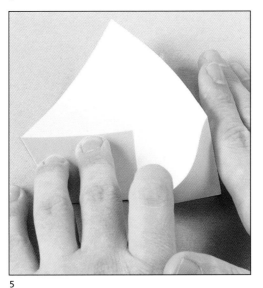

5

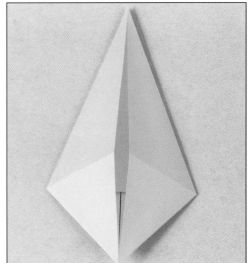

6

1

2

3

4

WATERBOMB BASE

MATERIALS

1 6in (15cm) square
(or as specified) from a sheet
of coloured paper

1 Start with the square of paper, white side facing upward, in a diamond shape. Fold the bottom point up to meet the top point to make the first diagonal line in the base. Unfold.

2 Turn the paper diamond around, so that this middle crease is now vertical. You now need to fold the paper in half once more, again taking the bottom point up to meet the top point to create the second, diagonal line. Unfold the paper once again, turn it over and then arrange in a square shape.

3 Book fold (*see p. 12*) the paper, taking the bottom edge up to meet the top edge and creasing in the horizontal line. All the creases should now meet in the middle of the paper. Turn over.

4 Take hold of the left- and right-hand edges of the paper with both hands just below the horizontal middle line. Start to push the sides in toward the middle section of the paper.

5 The paper begins to collapse into shape, but will not lie flat at this point.

5

6

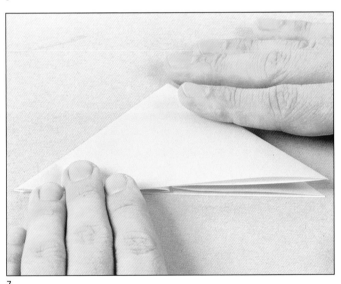

7

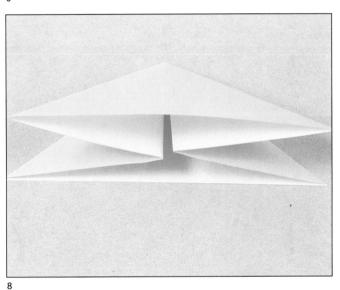

8

6 You need to keep pushing in the left- and right-hand sides of the paper, so that the lower half starts to go down and the paper begins to lie flat.

7 Flatten down the upper edge of the paper near the top point, so that it aligns neatly with the lower edge, forming a pyramid-shaped model.

8 The Waterbomb Base is now complete. You can see clearly the upper and lower layers with two flaps visible on both the right and left sides.

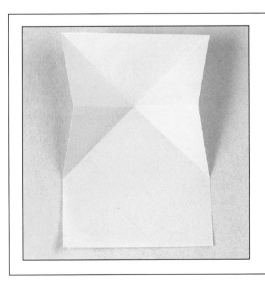

A WATERBOMB IN A RECTANGLE

When folding a Waterbomb Base in the top or bottom of a rectangular piece of paper (*see Angel pp. 64–65*), you need to treat it as a square and make sure that the horizontal crease that is made in Step 3 passes right through the intersection of the other two creases (see left). This helps to make sure the collapse of the paper in steps 4–7 is neat and precise.

TABLE DECORATIONS

1 Start with the square of patterned paper, white side facing upward. Fold the paper in half from left to right and top to bottom. Unfold.

2 Turn into a diamond shape and blintz fold (*see p. 12*) the corners to middle, where the creases meet.

3 Move paper to a square shape and turn over. Fold in half from bottom to top, creasing and unfolding. Turn around and fold bottom to top again, leaving paper folded in half. The blintzed flaps from Step 2 should be on the outside.

4 Unfold the paper and make a preliminary base (*see p. 14*) from new square formed in Step 2. When complete, the closed point of the base should be toward you.

5 The vertical middle line is made up of two outer edges, meeting at the middle. Separate these edges, place your fingers in the pockets underneath and hollow out the paper. Then bring the top point down and squash this flap into a bottom rectangle as shown. Repeat behind.

6 The tent shape from Step 5 has two flaps pointing to the left and two to the right. Take the top flap from the right and fold it to the left, using the vertical middle crease as an axis. Turn over and repeat.

7 Fold the new left- and right-hand edges formed in Step 6 inward to align with the vertical middle line. Turn over and repeat behind.

8 Fold down top point as far as it will go, until tip touches lower edge. Turn over and repeat behind.

9 Place fingers inside the hole at the top of model, pulling apart the flaps folded in Step 8. As you do this you can see the box shape appearing. Hollow out and shape box.

1

3

5

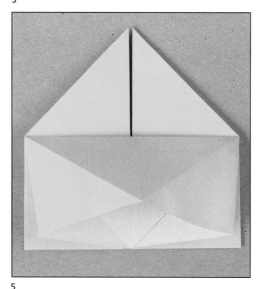

2

4

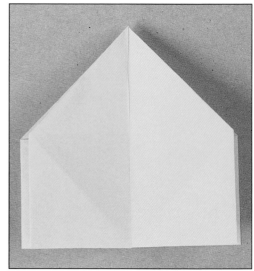

6

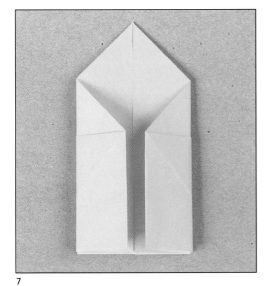

7

8

9

MATERIALS
(to make one box)
finished size: 1¾in x 1¾in x 1¾in (4.5cm x 4.5cm x 4.5cm)
1 6in (15cm) square
from a sheet of mediumweight
patterned paper

EASY LEVEL

JAPANESE BOX

Fill this attractive box with savoury snacks to start off a dinner party or with mini chocolate eggs to serve at a meal's end. It is a traditional model with uncertain origins, and the design has been passed down through many generations. This model is interesting in origami terms, as it is not until the final move when the flat folds are opened that the box shape appears. A 6in (15cm) square of paper makes a small box, so increase the size for a bigger box or boxes.

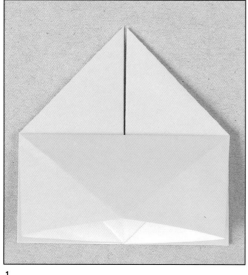

1

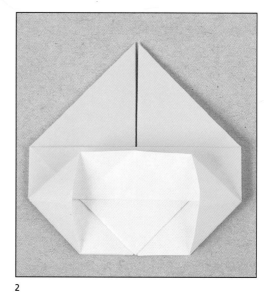

2

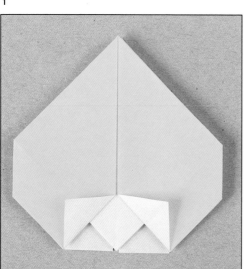

3

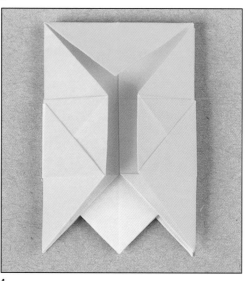

4

22

MATERIALS

(to make one box)

finished size: 1¾in x 1¾in x 1¾in (4.5cm x 4.5cm x 4.5cm)

1 6in (15cm) square from a sheet of mediumweight patterned paper

1 Start with Step 5 of the Japanese Box (*see pp. 20–21*) as shown.

2 Fold the bottom edge of the rectangle up to lie along the upper edge, folding the top layer only. To make the paper lie flat, you need to make two small triangular squash folds (*see p. 13*) at both the left-hand and the right-hand sides of the model. Turn the model over and repeat behind.

3 Continue folding as in Step 6 of the Japanese Box. Take the flaps along the lower edge at the base of the vertical middle line, and fold each

flap outward to form a right-angled triangle. Turn over and repeat.

4 In a similar way to the forming of the Japanese Box, fold the two outer vertical edges of the top layers inward to align with the vertical middle line. Fold top point down so upper sloping edges align with side flaps, then fold in this section over the outside edge of the box as far as it will go, as in Step 8 of the Japanese Box. Turn over and repeat behind with the second layer. To finish the model, open out and press it into shape as shown in Step 9 of the Japanese Box.

JAPANESE BOX WITH LEGS

To create a variation of a popular model, often only a few extra origami folds are needed. Here, the traditional Japanese Box on pages 20–21 is adapted with a few different folds into a box with legs.

This sophisticated-looking box can then be filled with sweets, mints, small macaroons or other delicacies and served with the coffee to make a stylish end to a dinner party. Make several boxes to impress your

guests if you are planning to entertain a large group of friends.

Fold the box in a mediumweight, good-quality, subtly patterned paper from a 6in (15cm) square if you just want to make a small box. For a larger size of box that will hold more sweets, just increase the size proportionately of the square you start folding with. If you want to make several boxes, buy a few sheets of the patterned paper in toning colours, so that you can add some interesting contrast and texture to your final table layout.

Although this box is simple to fold, take care to be accurate with your creases in steps 3 and 4, so that you produce neat, sharply folded legs for the box.

23

TABLE DECORATIONS

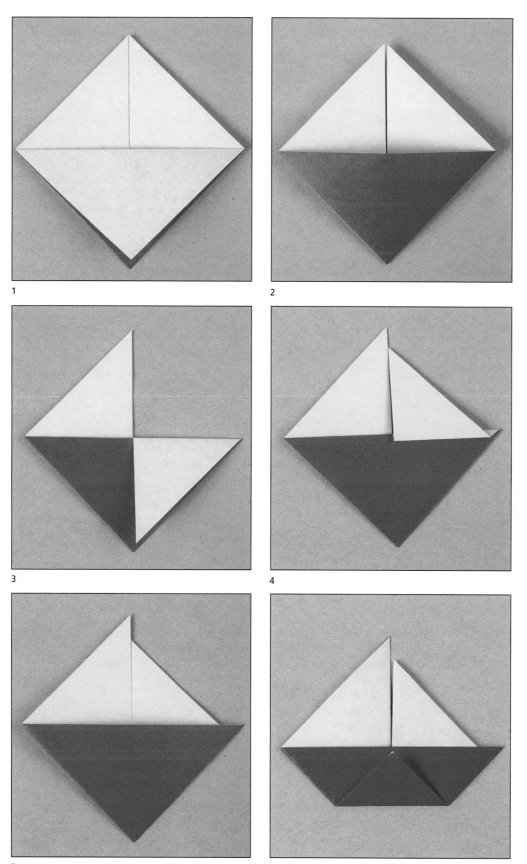

1

2

3

4

5

6

1 Start by making the preliminary base (*see p. 14*). Then place the base with the closed point toward you with the coloured side facing upward. Fold the top point downward to the closed point nearest you. Turn over and repeat behind.

2 Unfold these flaps, and using the same crease (the direction of which is reversed), mountain fold (*see p. 12*) the flap inside the model. You need to open the model out slightly to achieve this. Turn over and repeat behind.

3 Fold the top right point down to the closed point at the front, folding over the edge of what will be the boat's hull.

4 Using a crease parallel to, but slightly lower than, the crease made in Step 3, fold the same point back up on itself. This creates a thin, horizontal pleat in the paper, giving you a small sail.

5 Pull out the lower portion of the model (the hull), from beneath the pleat that was made in Step 4, allowing this pleat to tuck away neatly inside the hull.

6 Fold the closed point nearest you up to touch the horizontal top edge of the hull. If you unfold this flap to slightly less than 90° to the hull, the sailboat will stand up. Make other sailboats following the same method.

PARTY SAILBOAT

Liven up the table setting of a child's birthday party by using these colourful paper sailboats as place names. You can write each child's name across the boat's hull, so that each young guest can easily find their seats at tea time. Alternatively, you can use the sailboats as small party bags and fill them with an interesting selection of sweets for the children to take back home with them at the end of an enjoyable afternoon.

This traditional origami design of the sailboat has been revived by the American society of folding enthusiasts, Origami USA. The boat looks particularly striking when it is made from paper that has different, but toning, colours on each side. If you can't easily find this type of paper in stationery shops, you can always use some spray glue to fix two different-coloured sheets back to back.

The origami folds are simple to do as long as you take care with the folding. There is, however, one ingenious move that occurs in Step 5 that involves a pleat being tucked down inside the hull, making the small sail of the boat sink ingeniously right down inside it.

MATERIALS
(to make one sailboat)

finished size: about 4in x 3in (10cm x 7.5cm)

1 12in (30cm) square from a sheet of lightweight, two-coloured paper

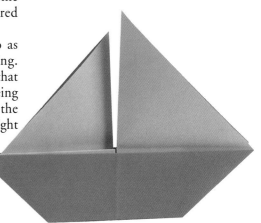

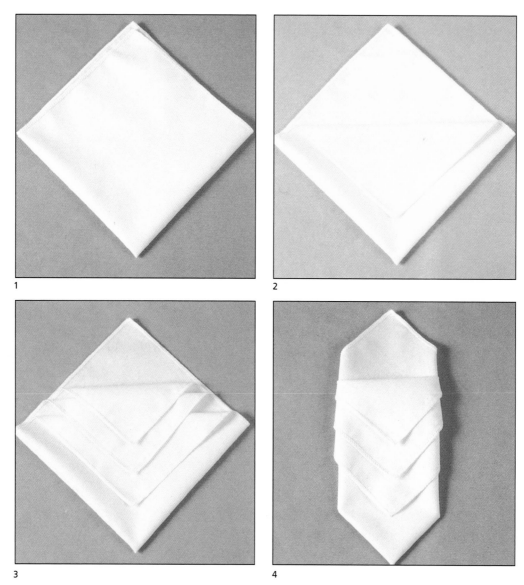

1

2

3

4

MATERIALS

(to make one buffet server)

1 starched white or
coloured cloth napkin

1 Start with the napkin folded into four, making sure that the four corners are all at the top. Turn the napkin around to make a diamond shape.

2 Fold one layer of the napkin down from the top point to slightly short of the bottom point and then carefully crease in a firm horizontal line.

3 Fold down the next layer of napkin, creasing in a horizontal line in exactly the same way, leaving a similar space between this layer and the first fold that was made.

Repeat this process with the third layer of the napkin.

4 Mountain fold (*see p. 12*) the left and right corners behind the napkin (these can meet in the middle or fall slightly short – it's entirely up to you). Tuck the items of cutlery into the little pouch at the front and then place the finished server in position on the table. Make as many other servers as are needed for your party guests in the same way.

BUFFET SERVER

This attractive napkin setting, which can hold up to three pieces of cutlery, is one of the most frequently used at large receptions and parties where large numbers of people are helping themselves to buffet food. It is a traditional origami design that is folded in a simple manner to achieve the pleasing layered effect. Make the server with a starched napkin, as this will help to keep the pleats firmly in position.

If you are planning a party for a large number of people, you can make the servers well in advance, folding several of them at one time. You can also use the server at more intimate dinner parties to impress your friends with your origami skills.

FLEUR-DE-LIS NAPKIN FOLD

Napkin folding can often seem a rather time-consuming process, but with this easy style you can soon liven up a dull table setting and feel inspired to go on and experiment with making more complex, demanding shapes. This traditional design works best with a starched napkin, as the stiff cloth helps to hold the final shape of the fleur-de-lis.

Take care when you are making the cylinder shape to allow sufficient napkin overlap, so that you can tuck one side neatly into the other.

If you want to make an alternative shape to the fleur-de-lis, you can just stop folding the napkin at Step 6 and leave it in the stylish shape of the bishop's mitre.

MATERIALS
(to make one napkin)

1 starched white or
coloured cloth napkin

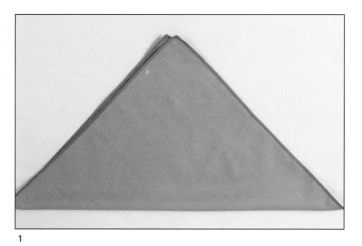
1

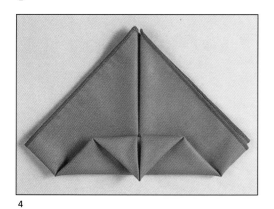
2

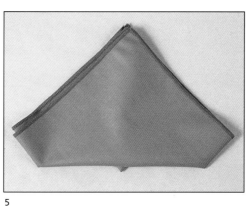
3

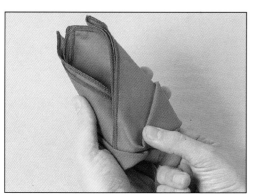
4

5

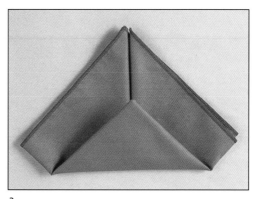
6

7

1 Place the napkin in a diamond shape and begin by folding it in half, taking the bottom point up to meet the top point.

2 Fold the two left- and right-hand points into the middle and up to reach the top point.

3 Fold the bottom point about threequarters of the way up, aligning it with the middle fold.

4 Fold the flap back down once more to touch the folded edge at the bottom.

5 Turn the napkin over, carefully holding all the folds together.

6 Bring the left- and right-hand corners together to form a cylindrical shape. Tuck the whole of one side into the pocket on the other side formed by the diagonal, folded edge. Push the napkin in deeply enough for the flap to hold in position. Reshape, then turn around to complete the bishop's mitre shape.

7 To make the fleur-de-lis shape, hold the mitre firmly in position at the base and join with your hand. Then pull gently on each of the loose flaps at the top of the mitre, peeling each one down in turn to form the side "feathers" as shown. Place the napkin on the table and make any other ones that you might need in the same way.

29

COMPARTMENT BOX

This type of box is so useful because you can store four separate items in the different compartments. It is perfect for holding different types of potpourri other natural ingredients. Alternatively, it can be served with a variety of cheese biscuits or chocolates at the end of a dinner party.

The base and lid of the box are a traditional "easy" box design, but the divider was created by Rachel Katz of the USA. Surprisingly, the three elements that make up the box are made from A4-sized paper. Just by folding the lid slightly differently, you can make it big enough to go on top of the base. Fold the box with a two-sided coloured paper or one with a toning reverse colour. For a bigger size, use a larger rectangle.

MATERIALS

finished size: 4¼in x 5½in x 2¼in (11cm x 14cm x 5.5cm)

3 A4-sized rectangles cut from a sheet of heavyweight, two-sided coloured paper

1

2

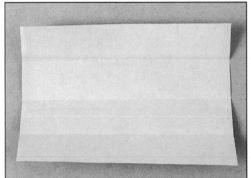

3

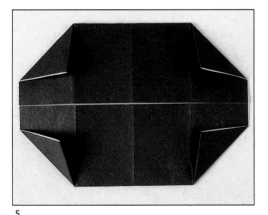

4

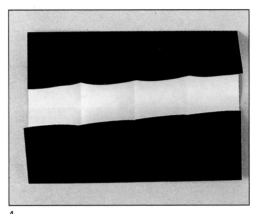

5

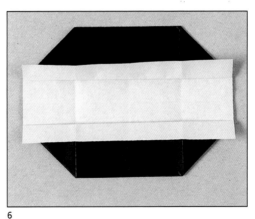

6

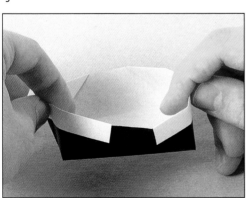

7

8

BASE

1 Start with first rectangle of paper with the longer edges horizontal. Book fold (*see p. 12*) in half, taking bottom edge up to meet the top edge. Unfold.

2 Fold each of the long edges inward, so that they align with the middle crease.

3 Unfold these flaps. The paper is now divided up into quarter sections horizontally.

4 Turn the paper around to make the short sides horizontal and repeat steps 1–2, but do not unfold.

5 Fold each corner of this new rectangle inward, so that the outer folded edges align with the light vertical creases.

6 Fold top and bottom flaps back on themselves, pressing them flat over the edges of the triangular flaps. This makes a parallel strip from right to left, as shown.

7 Place your fingers underneath these horizontal strips and into the pockets at the top and bottom. Pull gently open to create the shape of the base, allowing the left and right sides of the model to raise up along the creases.

8 Emphasize the shape of the base by running your fingers and thumbs along the outer dimensions, pinching the creases until the box is neatly formed.

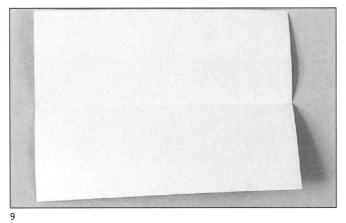

9

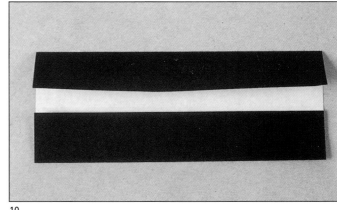

10

11

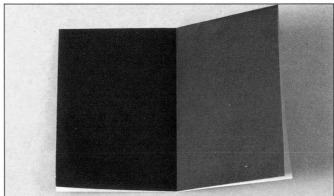

12

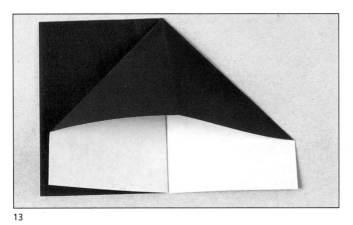

13

14

LID

9 Take second rectangle of paper, keeping long edges horizontal as before. Fold in half, from bottom to top. Unfold.

10 Fold the two long edges inward toward the horizontal middle line as before, but leave about ³⁄₁₆in (5mm) on both sides. Unfold both flaps.

11 Turn paper around to make short edges horizontal. Repeat steps 9–10, leaving same gap between outer edges and middle line. These creases make the box slightly longer and broader. Continue folding as for the base from steps 5–7 to finish lid. If too tight, just remake the lid with wider margins in steps 9–10; if it is too big just decrease the margins.

DIVIDER

12 Take the third rectangle of paper and make sure the short edges are horizontal. Fold the paper in half from right to left, then turn it around so that the crease just formed runs vertically. Fold in half again, but this time from bottom to top. Unfold, then turn the paper around so that the first crease now runs across the top.

13 Using vertical middle crease, raise right flap up to 90° to the rest of paper and squash fold (*see p. 13*) by placing fingers inside and pushing folded edge down flat as shown. Align this folded edge with the vertical middle line below.

14 Using vertical middle crease as an axis, take top flap at left and fold to right.

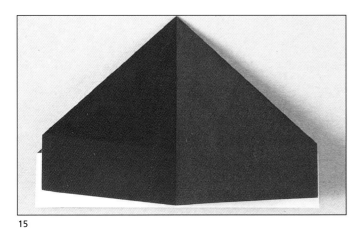

15

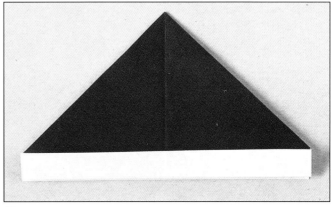

16

17

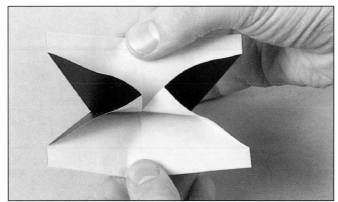

18

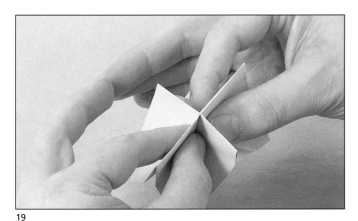

19

15 Repeat last step on left-hand flap. Take top right-hand flap of this squash fold and fold back to left to make a tent shape that is plain and smooth on each side.

16 Fold top layer of lower edge upward until lower corners left and right touch base of sloping sides to fold lower rectangle in half. Turn over and repeat.

17 Fold top point down to touch edge of strip formed in Step 15.

18 With your right hand take hold of the triangular flap and the layer beneath it, holding the lower layer firmly in place. Pull open the model, separating the two lower edges of the tent that was formed in Step 14. Holding the model away from you, mountain fold (*see p. 12*) the paper in half backward, using the vertical middle crease. You can now see four "compartments" starting to appear around a central cross shape.

19 Place your fingers and thumbs into these compartments, holding the model firmly as shown. Press down flat once again to establish the base crease required to keep the divider together. Place the divider inside the base of the box to keep its shape, then add the lid to complete the compartment box.

NAPKIN RING

Friends will be amazed by your origami skills when they see these delightful napkin rings adorning the tea table. You can make them from a mediumweight paper that is patterned both sides and which tones with the colour of your napkins. If you find patterned paper you like, but it is white on the reverse, you can stick a thin sheet of toning coloured paper on the back with some spray adhesive, if you prefer.

The origami technique used on this traditional design is called pleating, which features on some of the other projects included in the book. Fold the model carefully and accurately as the pleats need to be kept neat and even.

The opening steps of the project involve pre-creasing, where several folds are made and then unfolded, dividing the paper in many equal sections.

MATERIALS

(to make one napkin ring)

finished size: about 2½in (6.5cm) diameter ring

1 6in (15cm) square from a sheet of mediumweight, two-sided patterned paper

1 Start with the patterned square of paper, white side facing upward, in a diamond shape. Fold in half from left to right and bottom to top, folding and unfolding each time. Fold upper and lower points to the middle; unfold back to diamond.

2 Next fold each of the short points, first to the creases just made and then across the model to the same crease on the opposite side. Unfold once more to find that you have now divided the paper up into eight sections horizontally.

3 Turn the paper over. Working from the bottom upward, fold the lower point to the first, third, fifth and seventh intersections. Crease and unfold each time. Rotate the paper around so that the point at the top is now at the bottom. Fold as before, making sure you ignore the horizontal valley creases (see p. 12) just made. Check carefully that the space between the horizontal creases is equal. Fold and unfold as before, dividing the paper into sixteen sections horizontally.

4 Collapse the model by pleating the top and bottom corners in toward the middle, using existing valley and mountain creases (see p. 12). The middle diagonal stays unfolded.

5 Turn the model over and with the pleats on the outside, roll the paper into a circle. Bring the ends together and tuck the whole of one end inside the flaps at the other end. You may wish at this stage to use a round object such as a rolling pin to shape the napkin ring. Finally, using your fingers and thumbs, tease the napkin ring into the right shape. Make as many other napkin rings as are needed for the tea table using the same method.

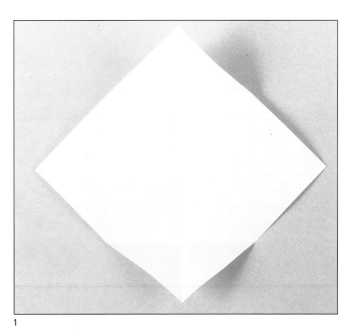

1

2

3

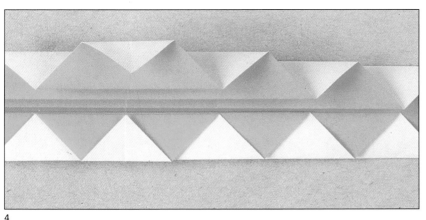

4

5

35

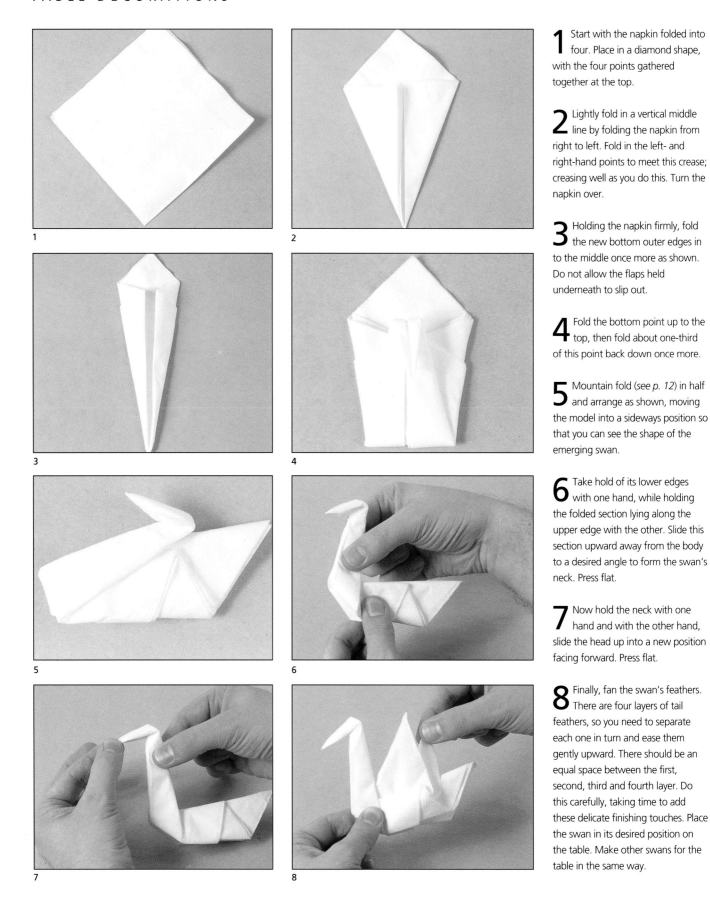

1 Start with the napkin folded into four. Place in a diamond shape, with the four points gathered together at the top.

2 Lightly fold in a vertical middle line by folding the napkin from right to left. Fold in the left- and right-hand points to meet this crease; creasing well as you do this. Turn the napkin over.

3 Holding the napkin firmly, fold the new bottom outer edges in to the middle once more as shown. Do not allow the flaps held underneath to slip out.

4 Fold the bottom point up to the top, then fold about one-third of this point back down once more.

5 Mountain fold (*see p. 12*) in half and arrange as shown, moving the model into a sideways position so that you can see the shape of the emerging swan.

6 Take hold of its lower edges with one hand, while holding the folded section lying along the upper edge with the other. Slide this section upward away from the body to a desired angle to form the swan's neck. Press flat.

7 Now hold the neck with one hand and with the other hand, slide the head up into a new position facing forward. Press flat.

8 Finally, fan the swan's feathers. There are four layers of tail feathers, so you need to separate each one in turn and ease them gently upward. There should be an equal space between the first, second, third and fourth layer. Do this carefully, taking time to add these delicate finishing touches. Place the swan in its desired position on the table. Make other swans for the table in the same way.

INTERMEDIATE LEVEL

SWAN NAPKIN FOLD

This delicate model makes a really beautiful decoration for a sophisticated table arrangement when you have invited some special dinner guests. It is a traditional design and can be successfully folded from both a paper (no more than double-ply) or a starched cloth napkin. If you make the swan from a cloth napkin, you can just place it on the dinner guests' side plates.

A good way of displaying a swan made from a paper napkin is to push the base of the swan's neck between the centre prongs of a fork. You can then lay the fork with the prongs upward on a side plate (see above). This helps to hold the shape together and also provides an elegant means of displaying the finished swan.

1 Start the model with the last step of the fish base (*see p. 15*) with the coloured side facing upward. Turn horizontally so that the sharp point is to the left. Valley fold (*see p. 12*) both flaps at the left across to the right to a point halfway between the right-hand point and the vertical crease as shown. Press flat.

2 Fold the top flap back on itself by approximately a third along the horizontal middle line.

3 Mountain fold (*see p. 12*) in half, placing the top portion behind the model.

4 Hold the model at the base (*see Step 6, p. 36*). Take hold of the swan's head and gently slide it upward and away from the body. Flatten into the new position to form the neck.

5 Hold the swan halfway up the neck, then slide the top away from the neck to form the head.

6 Fold the bottom corner upward to form half the stand and repeat behind. Adjust the angle of the stand if you want the swan to stand empty. Make other swans in the same way.

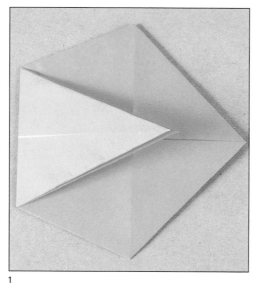

1

2

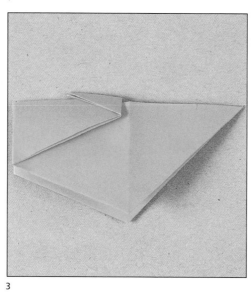

3

4

5

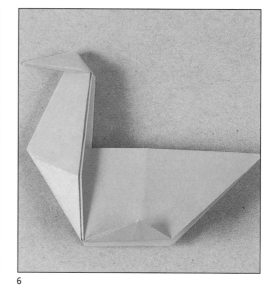

6

SWAN CANDY DISH

The stylish and elegant design of this dish is bound to impress all your dinner guests, and they will be even more amazed when they learn that you made it yourself. This traditional origami model has uncertain origins, but was introduced back into use recently by Laura Kruskal of the USA.

You can fold a large swan from a piece of mediumweight coloured paper (about 12in [30cm] square), fill it with dinner mints, and serve it to your guests with the·coffee after a dinner party. Alternatively, you can make several smaller swans from 6in (15cm) squares of paper, fill them with one or two mints or candies, and then position them at the side of each guest's place setting on the table.

The smaller swan is also ideal to hold mini chocolate eggs and can be put on the table for a special Easter lunch or tea.

If you just want to display the finished swan empty, adjust the fold of the crease of the stand until it will easily balance on its own. By placing some chocolates inside it, the swan will become stable.

Take your time with steps 4 and 5 of the project, as this is when you are forming the shape of the the swan's neck and head.

MATERIALS

(to make one swan)

finished size: 3¼ x 2¾in (8.5cm x 7cm)

1 6in (15cm) square from a sheet of mediumweight coloured paper

STAR BOX

This pretty box with its flaps in the shape of a star makes a delightful decoration for the table. You can fill it with some dried flowers or sweet-smelling potpourri and make it a centrepiece for the main table. Alternatively, place it on a coffee or side table filled with savoury snacks at a drinks party.

The model is a traditional design and is started from the Preliminary Base (*see p. 14*). Four squash folds (*see p. 13*) help to shape the side of the box. Fold the model carefully, creasing accurately, so that you make sure that all four points of the star box are neatly shaped and well formed. Use richly patterned paper which has a strong toning colour on the reverse to make the box. If you want a bigger size of box, just increase the size of the square detailed.

1 Start with the Preliminary Base (*see p. 14*) with coloured side of paper facing upward and the closed points facing toward you. Fold the upper sloping edge of the right-hand top flap inward to align with the vertical middle crease.

2 Raise the flap to 90° to the rest of the model, open out the paper along the long upper edges and squash fold (*see p. 13*), making sure that the folded edge lines up with the crease made in Step 1.

3 Repeat with the left flap. Turn the paper over and then repeat Step 2 with both flaps.

1

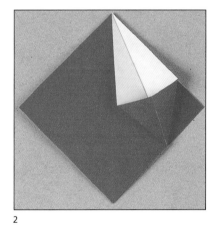

2

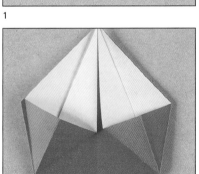

3

MATERIALS

finished size: the box has a base of about 4in (10cm) square

1 12in (30cm) square from a sheet of mediumweight paper, patterned one side and coloured on the other

4 Using the existing crease lines made in steps 2–3, fold the outer portion of each squash fold behind, tucking them in between the two flaps of the original Preliminary Base. Turn the paper over and repeat behind.

5 Fold the top point down as far as it will go. Turn the paper over and repeat behind.

6 Using the vertical middle crease as an axis, fold the top right flap across to the left. Turn the paper over and repeat this action behind. Now repeat Step 5 with these flaps on both sides.

7 To help shape the base of the box, fold up the bottom point to the crease connecting the left and right lower corners. To do this you must first temporarily unfold the top flap from steps 5–6. Crease the bottom point firmly.

8 Unfold the bottom point and fold the top point back down once more.

9 Open out the box by placing your fingers inside the hole running along the top edge of the model, while gently pulling the star flaps apart. Hollow out the box, pinching carefully around the base creases to make them firm.

4

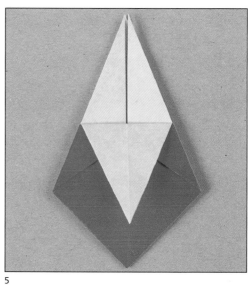

5

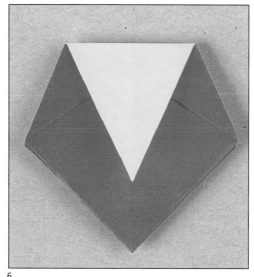

6

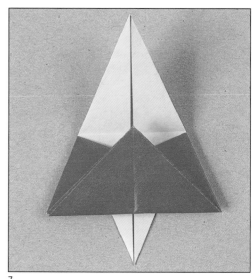

7

8

9

DISH

Make this charming dish from a brown or gray natural-looking textured paper and place it on a side table filled with nuts or exotic fruits. To make a larger dish, just increase the size of the starting square. The model was created by Eric Kenneway and was first published in *Origami 4* by Robert Harbin, who described the folding exercise as having a very pleasing sequence of folds that resulted in a sturdy, attractive dish.

Read the instructions and study the step-by-step pictures carefully, particularly when folding steps 9–13 where the layers are thick and quite difficult to do. These folds are made in "x-ray view", that is from the inside or going underneath an outer layer. This often occurs in origami and needs to be understood to be carried out correctly.

MATERIALS

finished size: about 5¾in x 5¾in x 1½in (14.5cm x 14.5cm x 3cm)

1 10½in (26cm) square from a sheet of heavyweight, two-sided brown, or gray textured paper

1 Start with the square of paper, coloured side facing upward, and book fold (*see p. 12*) in half from right to left. Unfold the paper, then fold the outer edges inward to align with the crease.

2 Turn paper over and, keeping creases vertical, fold outer folded edges inward to meet the vertical middle crease, allowing the flaps underneath to flip around and lie on top.

3 Turn paper over. Fold all the outer corners of vertical middle column inward to meet the middle crease. Then unfold top flaps only and lift the upper raw edge of the middle column. Then push the outer corners of flaps inward, turning them inside out.

4 Press the corners flat into their new position.

5 Take hold of the two top flaps at the back, either side of middle slit. Pull them apart slightly to stretch the middle point.

6 Keep pulling apart to flatten the middle point into a "bridge" between the two flaps.

7 Reinforce the new mountain crease (*see p. 12*) that is forming between outer flaps and push middle point back on itself and down inside the model. Allow the outer flaps to close again.

8 Press flat into new position. Then repeat steps 3–8 on bottom flaps from unfolding the top flaps sequence.

9 Mountain fold all the rear flaps either side of the middle slit outward, so that the horizontal edges at the top and bottom now align with the outer vertical edges of the model.

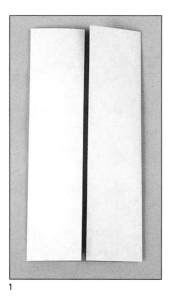

1

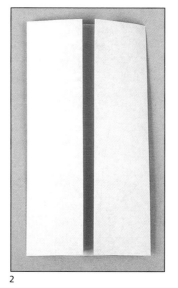

2

3

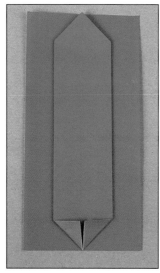

4

5

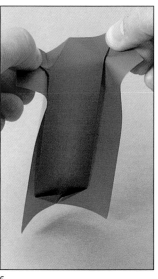

6

7

8

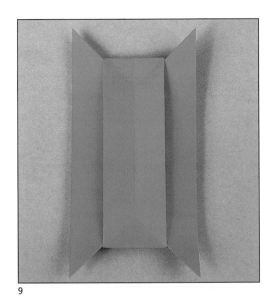

9

10

10 Fold top corners down on the hinge crease at the base of the flaps, so that the tips align with the outer vertical edges as shown. Lift up the vertical middle column slightly as the flaps slide down. Repeat at the bottom.

11 Fold the tips of the flaps back inward, so that the outer vertical edges align with the horizontal crease every time. Then tuck the flaps right under the middle vertical column.

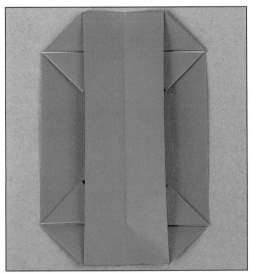

11

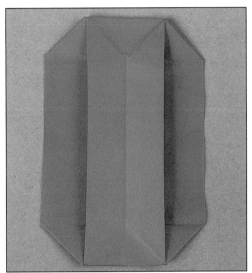

12

12 Fold the small triangular flaps outward on the horizontal hinge creases, tucking them into the corner pockets either side of the middle column. As in Step 10, the crease is in "x-ray" of the middle portion of paper.

13 Turn paper over and fold middle vertical folded edges outward to align with vertical outer edges. These creases are made in x-ray of horizontal flaps at top and bottom. Fold through all the layers.

13

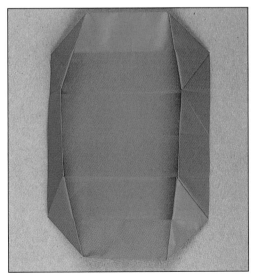

14

14 Turn the model over, keeping the same way up. Open out the two vertical side flaps until flat to the working surface. The horizontal edges at top and bottom will fold inward and squash flat. Reverse the process, lifting the horizontal flaps so that the vertical sides fold in. With all sides equal, the dish is complete.

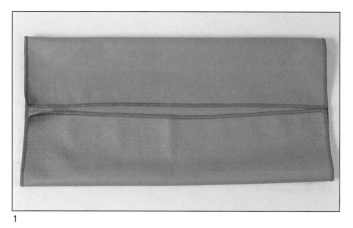

1

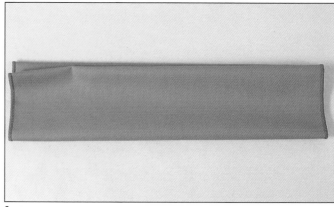

2

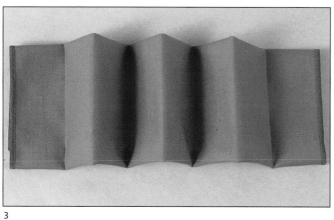

3

4

5

6

1 Fold a horizontal middle crease in the napkin. Unfold, then book fold (see p. 12) the top and bottom edges in to meet this crease.

2 Fold in half, bringing the bottom edge up to meet the top edge.

3 You now need to divide the napkin into eighths, vertically using alternate valley and mountain creases (see p. 12). First fold the left edge across to the right to make the vertical middle crease. Unfold. Next fold the two outer edges in to align with this crease, so that you now have quarters. Unfold, and turn over, keeping same way up. Make forward folds in between the existing creases to divide the napkin into eight. To do this, first fold in each outer edge to align with the nearest crease. Unfold.

Then fold outer edges across to this same point, only on the opposite side (the threequarter crease), folding and unfolding each time.

4 Collapse all the creases into a fan, then pinch at the base allowing all the layers to spread open.

5 On one side of the fan, carefully separate the double thickness of

layers at the top. Then, between each pleat, pull down each edge to form a triangular bridge between the pleats creating valley creases. Continue like this to complete one side.

6 Repeat on other side of fan making alternate pleats as before. Allow the napkin to open, each end falls gently onto the table. Make other napkins in the same way.

DOUBLE FAN NAPKIN FOLD

Here, a beautiful, traditional napkin fold, which is often featured by restaurants to decorate their tables, can look equally good placed on your dinner table at home. Match or contrast the colour of your napkins to your dinner service, so that they really stand out and make a striking impact on the table.

It is best to use a starched cloth napkin when folding, so that the fan shape you create will stay neatly in place.

Folding in the pleated design is quite difficult to do and it takes some practice to achieve properly, so don't worry if your first napkin is not quite right and does not seem to fall in the correct way.

You also need to be patient when you push in the layers to create the scalloped effect of the fan.

If you are planning to make several double fan napkins for a large dinner party, start making them the night before the meal so that you allow yourself plenty of time to rectify any mistakes and to get all the folds shaped exactly as you want them on your finished napkins.

This napkin design might be time consuming to make, but the final effect is well worth the effort.

MATERIALS
(to make one napkin)

1 starched white or colouredcloth napkin

CHRISTMAS DECORATIONS

1 Start with the square of paper, coloured side facing upward. Fold the paper in half, bringing the bottom edge up to meet the top edge. Unfold and turn the paper around so that the crease is vertical.

2 Fold the bottom edge of the paper up by a small amount to form a thin parallel border.

3 Turn the paper over, keeping the white strip running horizontally along the bottom edge. Fold the left- and right-hand edges inward to align with the vertical middle line.

4 Turn the model around so that the white strip is at the top. Fold in the bottom left- and right-hand corners to align with the vertical middle line.

5 Fold the bottom point up to touch the top edge of the flaps folded in Step 4.

6 Fold the model in half, taking the bottom edge up to meet the top edge.

7 As shown in the picture, fold the upper portion of the model back down on itself, aligning the corners at the base of the sloping edges with the lowest corners.

8 Fold the model in half from right to left along the middle crease.

9 Hold the back of the stocking about halfway up with one hand, while holding the toe with the other. Slide the toe out in front, opening out the pleat at the rear of the heel. Flatten into position.

10 Open out the back of the stocking slightly, then re-fold, tucking upper flap under edge of white strip of the flap underneath. Make other stockings in the same way.

1

2

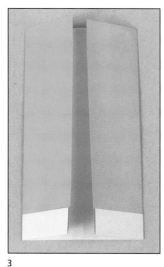

3

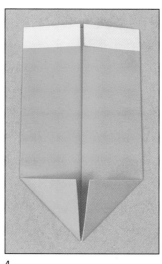

4

5

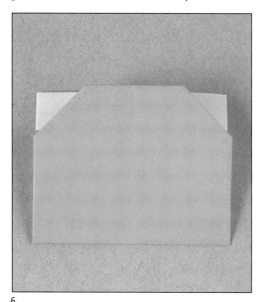

6

7

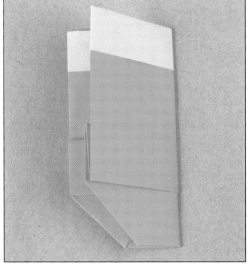

8

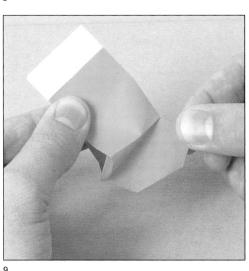

9

10

CHRISTMAS STOCKING

Fill up this sturdy little stocking with sweets and candy sticks to delight a child on Christmas morning. Pop it in a pillowcase with other presents, or make several stockings and hang them on the Christmas tree.

This traditional origami design is easy to make and you can have great fun swivelling the toe of the stocking forward in Step 9. Use red or festive paper with a white backing which then forms the stocking trim.

MATERIALS
(to make one stocking)

finished size: about 5¼in x 2¼in (13.5cm x 5.5cm)

1 9in (22.5cm) square from a sheet of mediumweight, one-sided red or festive paper

51

EASY LEVEL

SIX-POINT STAR

Stars are one of the most popular decorations to make for Christmas, and this simple star model is a project that can be easily taught to children. It can feature in a nativity scene on a dark-blue background, or several can be strung together as a separate decoration.

There are other methods of making the equilateral triangle that is the basis of the star, but steps 1–4 show one of the easiest. To make bigger stars, just increase the size of the square of paper detailed.

MATERIALS
(to make one star)

finished size: 3½in x 3in (9cm x 7.5cm)

1 6in (15cm) square from a mediumweight sheet of foil gift-wrap paper

1 Start with the square of paper, coloured side facing downward, and fold in half from bottom to top. Turn the paper around so that the crease runs vertically on the left.

2 Fold back one layer of the top right-hand corner to align with the folded left edge and to run down to the bottom right-hand corner.

3 Cut along the edge of the flap formed in Step 2, separating the coloured section from the white section of the paper.

4 Open out the lower portion of paper to form an equilateral triangle. Discard the rest of the paper. Start folding the star with the coloured side face up.

5 The triangle already has the first middle crease. Similar creases are needed that extend from the remaining points. Make these by folding the triangle in half twice, first bringing the top point down to the right-hand point and then bringing it down again to the left-hand point. Fold and unfold each time.

6 Fold in all three points of the triangle to the middle point where the creases that were made in Step 5 intersect.

7 Unfold back to the triangle and turn paper over. Fold down the top point to the lower edge, lining up with the vertical middle crease.

8 Fold this point back upward once more, using the crease made in Step 6.

9 Repeat steps 7 and 8 with the remaining two triangular points, turning them round each time to make an equilateral triangle again.

10 Steps 7 and 8 make a pleat across each point of the triangle, with the last to be folded lying on top. To "lock" the model in position, lift up the corner of the first pleat and tuck the similar corner of the last underneath, as shown. This places each pleat alternately under and over its neighbour.

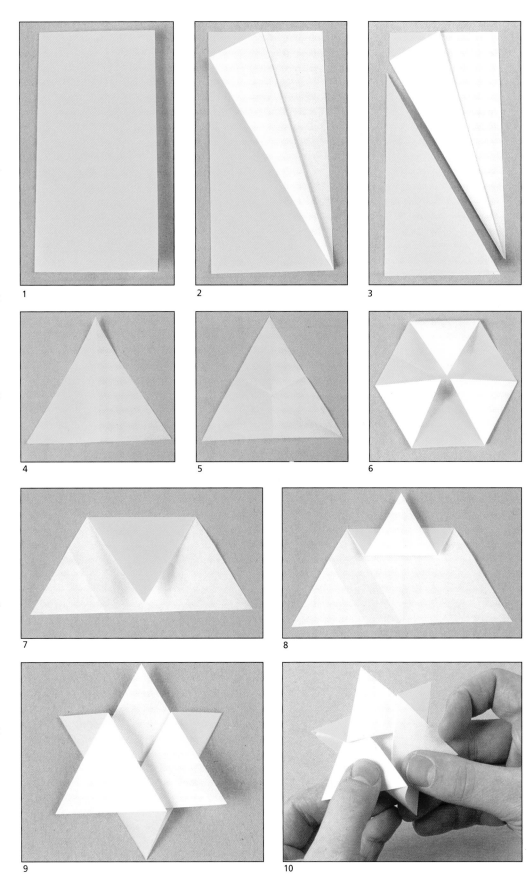

1

2

3

4

5

6

7

8

9

10

1 Start with the square of paper, coloured side facing upward in a diamond shape. Fold the paper in half from bottom to top. Unfold and turn the paper around so that the middle crease is vertical. Fold in left- and right-hand points close to the middle crease. Then fold down the top point to meet the middle vertical line, as shown. Note the position of all the flaps which can be adjusted.

2 Mountain fold (see p. 12) the left-hand side of the paper to make the first bird that faces left. To make the second bird that faces right, mountain fold the right-hand side of the paper.

3 Hold the model about halfway down, then take hold of the upper white flap, sliding it outward away from the body as shown. Flatten it into this new position to create the head.

4 Mountain fold the lower point of the paper upward to come behind the crease running along the edge of the white flap, which is the bird's wing.

5 Finish the model by folding back the lower point to shape the body and tail. Pleat the head with small mountain and valley pleats (see p. 12) at the top of the bird's head to make its beak. Finally, fold back the point at the back of the robin's head to finish. Make the second bird to face the other way with the second square of paper. When both birds are complete, fold the A4 card in half from top to bottom and arrange the robins in position in your desired design. When you're happy with their position, fix them in place with the paper glue.

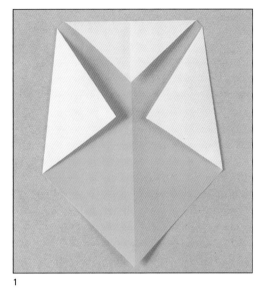

1

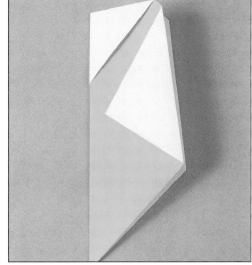

2

3

4

5

MATERIALS

finished size of robins: about 3⅛in x 1¾in (8cm x 4.5cm)

2 4½in (11.5cm) squares from a sheet of lightweight red paper

1 A4-sized rectangle cut from a sheet of white or buff cartridge paper

Paper glue

ROBIN CARD

Christmas is a time for keeping in touch with old friends and an ideal way of doing this is to send them your own handmade Christmas cards. The robins on the card are the author's creation and are very simple to make. By using a 6in (15cm) square of red paper you can make a bird to fit on a folded

A4 size white or buff card. The second robin, that faces the other way, is also easy to make and only requires a slightly different fold in Step 2.

If you want to make a smaller card (about A5 size), just reduce the size of the square of paper for folding to 4½in (11.5cm) to give you the smaller robins as shown above.

Don't worry if each robin that you make looks different because, as you are "free folding" and not working to precise measurements, no two birds will ever end up looking exactly the same.

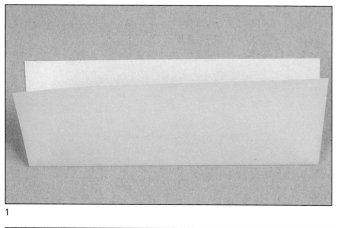

1

2

3

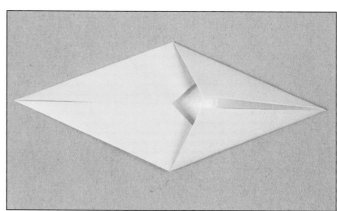

4

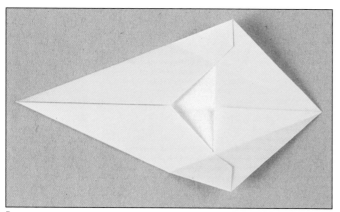

5

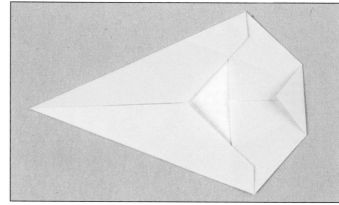

6

1 Start with the coloured green rectangle, white side facing upward, with the long edges horizontal. Fold the paper in half, bringing the bottom edge up to meet the top edge.

2 Unfold, and then fold in the four corners to align with the horizontal middle crease that was made in Step 1.

3 Fold in the lower left outer sloping edge so that it aligns with the horizontal middle crease made in Step 1.

4 Repeat Step 3 with the upper right sloping edge, then apply the same folding technique to the two remaining edges at the right. The flaps formed will then overlap both the left flaps.

5 Unfold the flaps on the right as folded in Step 4.

6 Fold the right-hand point inward to just under halfway along the triangular flaps. Align it with the horizontal middle crease.

7 Refold the two right flaps back to the horizontal middle crease, using the creases made in Step 4.

8 Fold the right-hand edge across to the left, making a vertical valley crease (*see p. 12*) that then connects the upper and lower corners at the middle.

9 Fold the top portion back across to the right, so that a small amount of paper projects beyond the folded edge underneath. This forms the pot, the size of which can be

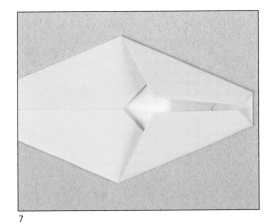

7

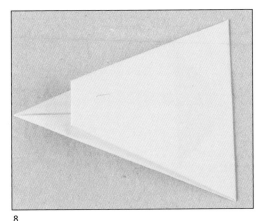

8

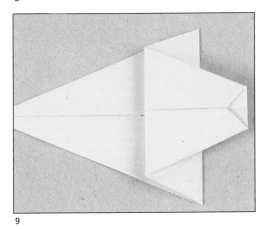

9

altered by the position of the above
crease. Turn the model over to finish
the tree. Fold the A4 card in half from
left to right and glue on the tree.
Decorate it with the glitter, metallic
pens or foil circles to suit the look you
want to achieve. To finish, draw a
freehand star on top of the tree using
the gold or silver metallic pens. Make
as many other cards as you need
using the same method.

CHRISTMAS TREE CARD

Surprise your friends and family next
Christmas by sending them your own
handmade cards. This traditional Christmas tree design is not difficult to make, but
you will be surprised by how cleverly the
tree's pot is formed by the folds in Step 9.

Make the tree from green paper and glue
it onto some cream or white card. Once it is
fixed to the card, you can decorate the tree
in many different ways: you can glue some
glitter on it, draw on ornaments with gold
and silver metallic pens, or glue on some
baubles made by punching out coloured
foil circles with a hole punch.

MATERIALS
(to make one card)

finished size of tree: about 3½in (9cm) high

1 A6-sized rectangle cut from a sheet of dark-green mediumweight paper

1 A4-sized rectangle cut from a sheet of white or cream cartridge paper

Paper glue

Glitter, gold and silver metallic pens, coloured foil circles to decorate

1 Start with the square of paper, white side facing upward, in a diamond shape. Fold from bottom to top, turn until the crease is vertical, and fold in the same way again.

2 Blintz (*see p. 12*) all corners to the middle point, then turn the paper over.

3 Take hold of the bottom edge and fold it in to meet the horizontal middle crease. Allow the blintzed flap from Step 2 to flip around to the front and open out. Repeat with the top edge.

4 Fold the small triangles at the right over the edge of the central square to align with the horizontal middle line. Repeat this procedure on the left.

5 Now unfold these small triangles from Step 5 and refold, this time, tucking them away underneath the central square to hold them in place. Each half of this central square has to be lifted up slightly to accomplish this.

6 Two folded edges meet to form the horizontal middle line. Separate these edges, and then place your fingers inside the model and hollow out the inner pockets to form a square and shape the crown.

7 Press and model the crown further to emphasize its square shape, especially at the corners. Make other crowns as needed using the same method.

1

2

3

4

5

6

7

CROWN PARTY HAT

MATERIALS
(to make one party hat)

1 sheet of gold or silver gift-wrap paper, cut into a square

Christmas is the time for parties and wearing paper hats, so now you can delight your friends by making this crown party hat. This traditional crown design is also ideal for children's parties. As people's heads vary, it is hard to give standard sizes for the hat. A rough guide is that a hat made from a sheet of gift-wrap paper, cut into a square, should fit an adult. For a child, trim two adjacent sides of the square by 3–4in (7.5cm–10cm).

(to make one teardrop)

**finished size: 3in
(7.5cm) high**

1 6in (15cm) square from a
sheet of lightweight origami
or ordinary foil paper

Gold thread

Glue

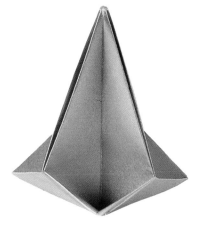

INTERMEDIATE LEVEL

TEARDROP
ORNAMENT

Everybody loves a decorated tree at Christmas
and by making several of this pretty ornament
you'll make it look even more attractive. Its
three-dimensional design was created by Rae
Cooker, an American. Take care when folding
the teardrop as there are so many squash folds
(*see p. 13*) at the end. The ornament looks
spectacular made from origami foil paper,
which is white on one side and has four quarters of different coloured foil on the other.

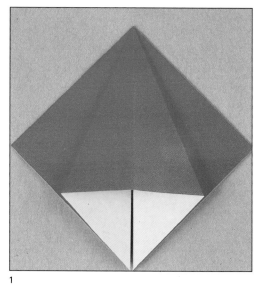

1

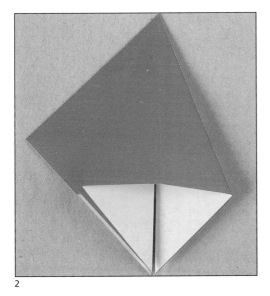

2

3

4

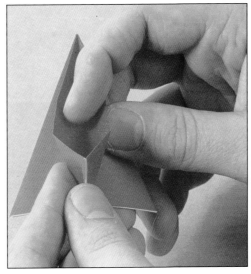

5

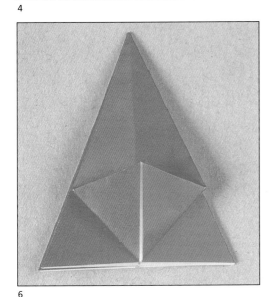

6

7

1 Start by making the Preliminary Base (*see p. 14*). Then place the base with the coloured side facing upward, with the closed point at the top end. Perform squash folds (*see p. 13*) on each of the four flaps of this base. Do this by raising the top flap at the right, so that it stands at 90° to the rest of the model, using the vertical middle crease as an axis. Squash fold the flap. Turn the paper over and repeat on the other side.

2 Now perform squash folds on the remaining two flaps. First fold the right side of the kite shape across to the left using the vertical middle crease so that you can squash fold the right-hand flap.

3 Turn the model over and repeat Step 2 on remaining flap of the Base. The model is now symmetrical with two flaps to the left and two to the right. Fold the lower flap at the right upward as far as it will go, so that the small triangle lies on top of the larger one. Repeat at left side and then repeat with flaps behind.

4 Unfold flaps and re-fold, tucking them up inside the model under lower edge of big triangle.

5 Now perform squash folds on all four flaps in a similar way to steps 1–3, but this time separate the upper edges of each flap. Make sure that you hold the model firmly to the surface you are working on, so that the paper layers don't spring apart.

6 Flatten down the squash fold to complete. Repeat with the three remaining flaps.

7 To make the teardrop three dimensional, hold the top of the model while carefully opening out the squash folds made in Step 6. To hang on a tree, glue some gold thread to top of model. Make other teardrops using the same method.

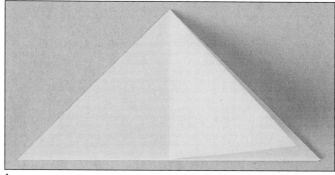

1

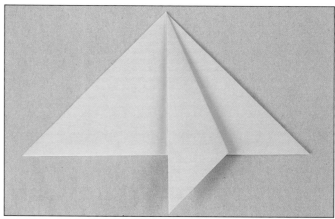

2

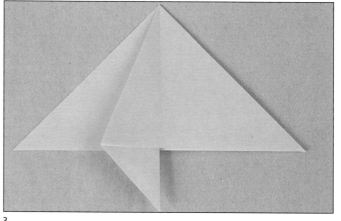

3

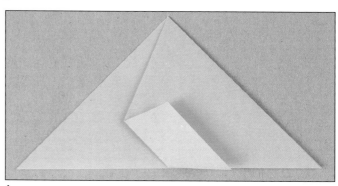

4

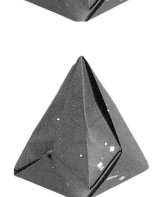

FESTIVE BELL

Three-dimensional decorations are quite tricky to make in origami, but the finished effect is well worth it. This charming bell really stands out when placed among the other decorations on the Christmas tree. Once you've mastered the folding technique you can make several bells and place them in different positions on the tree.

The model is designed by Paul Jackson of the UK and has an interesting finale when the model is slightly inflated by blowing through the hole at the bottom of the bell. Ideally, use foil paper, but when folding it, make sure that you do not fold too neatly or you will close off the bottom hole.

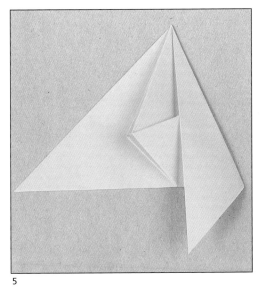

5

6

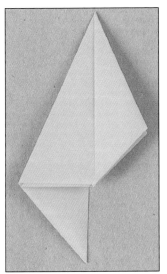

7

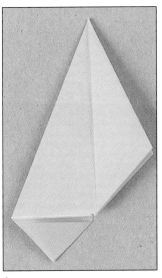

8

9

10

11

3 Fold this half-kite-shaped flap across to the left, using the vertical middle crease as the axis.

4 Fold lower portion of flap back up toward the right, so that the bottom point aligns with the pyramid's bottom edge.

5 Fold the top flap at the right as detailed in Step 2, so that the outer sloping edge aligns with the vertical middle crease.

6 Repeat steps 2–5 with the next two flaps. To make it easier to do this, take the rear flap at the left and fold it behind to the right on the middle crease to spread the paper layers evenly.

7 Repeat Step 2 with the final right-hand flap, then turn model over from right to left, keeping it the same way up.

8 Fold bottom point up to touch the left corner.

9 Fold the lower-left portion up and across to the right, matching the crease with the folded edge behind it. The flap now aligns with the lower-right edge. Tuck this under the folded edge of the right-hand pocket side.

10 To shape the bell, fold the upper portion over the edge of the thicker lower portion, creasing firmly between outer edges and the vertical·middle line. Fold and unfold in both directions, then turn model over and repeat behind, so that the creases flex both ways.

11 Hold bell at the bottom and spread the four side flaps apart. Inflate the bell by blowing into the base's hole. To hang on the tree, glue some gold thread to the top of the model. Make other bells using the same method.

MATERIALS

(to make one bell)

finished size: 3in (7.5cm) high

1 6in (15cm) square of lightweight foil paper

Gold thread

Glue

1 Start with the Waterbomb Base (*see p. 16*) with closed point away from you. Using the middle line as an axis, fold top left flap across to right.

2 Fold the outer sloping edge of this flap inward to align with this vertical middle crease.

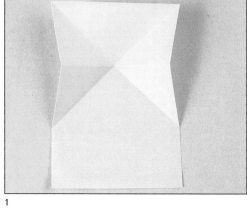

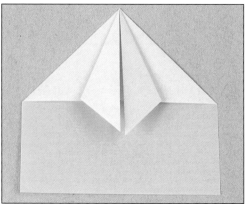

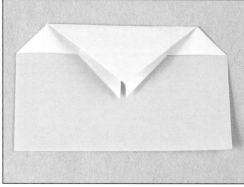

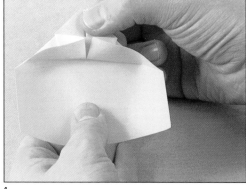

finished size: about 4¾in x 2¼in (12cm x 5.5cm) from A5

1 A5 or A6-sized rectangle cut from a sheet of lightweight, good-quality white or cream cartridge paper

Glue (optional)

Gold thread (optional)

INTERMEDIATE LEVEL

ANGEL

This stunning Christmas decoration can be made from an A5 rectangular sheet of cartridge paper so that it is large enough to sit on top of the Christmas tree, or it can be made smaller from an A6 sheet and hung with gold thread as another tree decoration.

The angel model was designed by David Brill of the UK, who is a very popular and influential creator of origami. Often in origami a fold can be made in what has become termed "to taste". Step 9 of this model is such an occasion and it determines whether you make a rahter thin or a more rounded angel model.

1 Start with long edges of the rectangle vertical. Fold a Waterbomb Base at the top of the paper (see p. 17).

2 Fold the outer sloping edges of the pyramid's top flaps inward to align with middle line.

3 Fold down top point of middle kite shape to bottom point of the flaps just made, creasing carefully to prevent lower flaps sliding out.

4 Take hold of all the flaps and pull back open, returning them to a position similar to Step 2.

5 Now make two small squash folds (see p. 12) in the lowest paper layer so that it lies flat.

6 Press down well to complete the folds.

7 Take hold of the "loose" flap at the top right of the model, then holding the left side firmly with your other hand, slide this flap outward to the right into a new position.

8 Flatten all layers into this new position. If necessary, realign the paper around the middle crease for a neat model. Repeat at left.

9 Turn model over. Fold the left portion about halfway across the model "to taste". Make the crease a little way down the outer sloping edge to give the angel a tapering body.

10 Repeat with the right flap, overlapping it with the left. To finish, fold top point down on a crease connecting the two creases made in Step 9 to suggest a head. Fold excess paper at front behind to finish level with lower edge of "gown" behind. Finally, pleat wings by folding tips back and forth. For a small angel, glue on thread to hang on the tree.

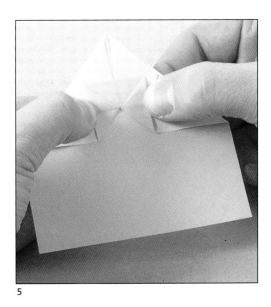

5

6

7

8

9

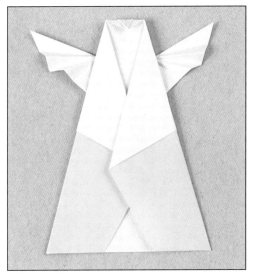

10

1 Start with the preliminary base (*see p. 14*) with the coloured side facing upward and the closed points at the top. Make squash folds (*see p. 13*) on all the flaps to make them kite shaped. When the model is symmetrical, fold the right-hand corner of the upper kite-shaped flap across to the left, revealing a smooth, plain surface (*see steps 1 and 2 pp. 60–61*). Turn the paper over and repeat behind.

2 Fold the outer sloping edges inward by a small amount, giving a long thin triangular flap each side. Note the crease begins at the top point and the left and right flaps need to be folded equally.

3 Using the vertical middle crease as an axis, work around the layers performing Step 2 wherever there is a smooth, plain face, to make the model symmetrical again.

4 Fold the bottom corner up to touch the horizontal edges of the flaps squashed in Step 1, just visible through the upper layer of paper. Again, using the vertical middle crease as an axis, work around the layers, repeating this step on similar sides.

5 Fold the lower sloping edges inward to align with the vertical middle crease. Again, repeat three more times on the remaining flaps.

6 Fold the lower portion of the paper upward as far as it will go, then mountain fold (*see p. 12*) the tip behind and into the pocket formed by the two side flaps folded in Step 5. Again, repeat all the way around the model to the similar sides. Then place your fingers inside the hole at the base of the model and carefully hollow out the hat, making sure to open out all the little corners to make a beautiful rounded shape. Make any more hats that are needed using the above method.

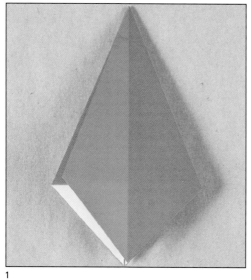
1

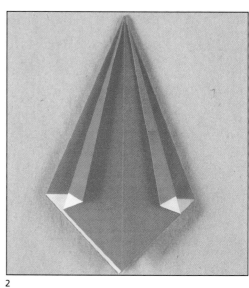
2

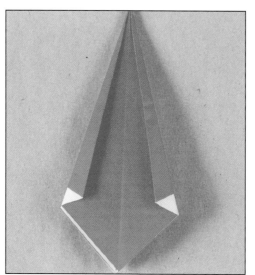
3

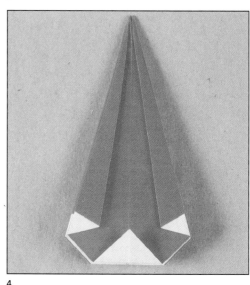
4

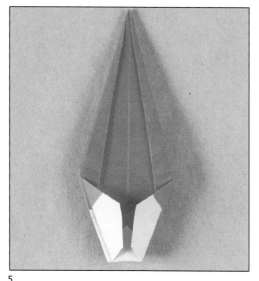
5

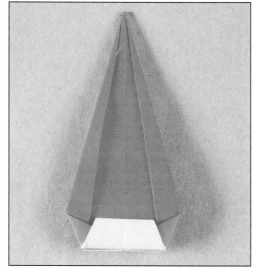
6

CHINESE PARTY HAT

Children will love to wear this hat at a Christmas party or to be one of the Wise Men in the school nativity play. It can also be worn as part of a Chinese outfit by adults going to a fancy dress party.

The hat is designed by an Austrian folder, Christoph Mangutsch and it is folded first from the Preliminary Base (*see p. 14*). You need to fold carefully, following a similar sequence of repetition around all the flaps. This design requires extreme precision in the folding and similar care needs to be taken when opening out the hat, so that you do not lose the creases when you want to wear it.

Experiment first with a large square cut from a sheet of tabloid newspaper (*see p.59*), trimming the ends further or making another larger square, until you find the right size of hat for the average adult head.

For children you will need to experiment further by trimming down the square on both sides until you find the right basic size for their age group.

Strong, brightly coloured, heavyweight paper is the best type to use, so that the hat will hold its shape well and not tear.

67

MATERIALS
(to make one parcel)

1 sheet of coloured gift-wrapping paper for parcel

1 small label cut from a sheet of coloured gift-wrap paper

1 thin strip of ribbon cut from a sheet of coloured gift-wrap paper

Scissors

ADVANCED LEVEL

GIFT-WRAPPED PARCEL

Giving Christmas presents to friends or relatives that have been packaged specially using origami folds is bound to delight them. This gift-wrap design is the author's creation and is based on ideas by Paul Jackson and Kunio Ekiguchi. To make a rectangular package you need three different-coloured papers. The first rectangular sheet is the main wrapping paper, and should be longer and wider than the gift, after the paper is pleated. A small label is needed from the second sheet of paper. Finally, cut a thin paper strip from the third sheet for the ribbon – about 2¼in (6cm) is the right width if the present is wrapped in a sheet of gift-wrap.

1

2

3

4

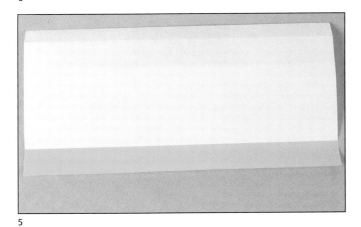

5

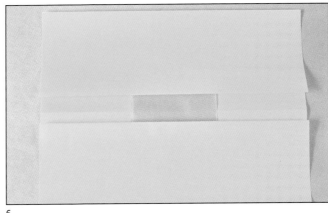

6

1 With the white side of the paper for the parcel facing upward, fold the paper in half away from you bringing the bottom up to the top, so that the coloured side is now on the outside and the fold is facing toward you.

2 Fold the lower edge of the paper upward about one-third of the way, as shown. Make a sharp crease, then unfold the paper completely, keeping all the folds horizontal. The lowest crease should be a mountain fold (*see p. 12*).

3 Keeping the coloured side of the paper facing upward, place the second piece of paper, the label, centrally on the paper. This label needs to be shorter in width than the gift and should fit neatly in the space created between the outer creases, as shown above.

4 Now take hold of the paper at the lower crease, pinch it carefully between your fingers and thumbs, then slide this lower portion slowly upward until it reaches the label. Check underneath that the pleat you have created is neat and even all the way along.

5 Next, fold the top edge of the paper down over the edge of the label until it nearly reaches the end of the paper, as shown, and crease this fold well.

6 Fold the top flap back up again on the original crease from Step 2 to create the second pleat, then turn the paper over, holding the label firmly in position.

7 Place the gift on the paper, making sure that it is right in the middle.

8 Wrap the left- and right-hand sides in over the gift, interlocking the pleats as shown, and carefully pull taut.

9 Close off the ends of the parcel by folding in the excess paper conventionally. Trim the ends first if they are too long.

10 The final piece of paper, the ribbon, needs to be long enough to go once around the package from label to label. Begin by tucking one end of the ribbon, white side up, under and inside one of the pleats on top of the label.

11 Fold the ribbon back on itself so that the coloured side is wrapped around the gift. Crease, and then pull the ribbon under the package and over the other side.

12 Tuck the remaining end of the ribbon under the other pleat. If it is too long, trim it first, then insert in place to make a neat and tidy parcel.

7

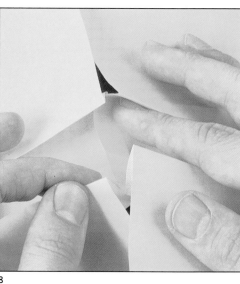

8

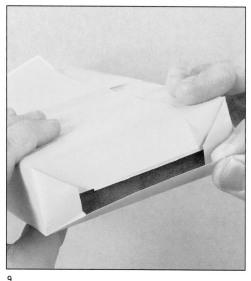

9

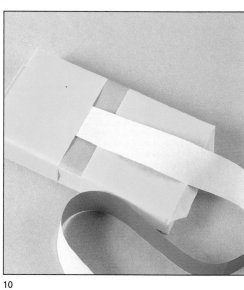

10

11

12

HAPPY SANTA GIFT TAG

Christmas is a time for giving presents and now you can liven up an ordinary parcel by gluing this jolly gift tag on the front. The tag is quite straightforward to make, but does involve several folding stages that need to be followed carefully so that you make an accurate model.

Designed by John Smith, a leading origami expert, the model uses only valley folds (*see p. 12*), which is a style that has come to be recognized as "pure" origami. By making the Santa from one-sided red paper, the white reverse side is then cleverly used to make the beard, facial features and also the decorative hat trim.

1

2

3

4

5

6

7

8

9

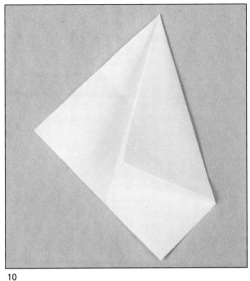

10

11

12

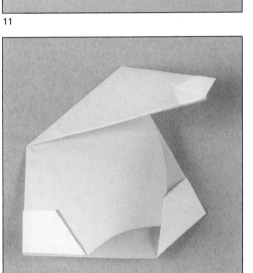

13

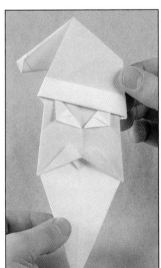

14

MATERIALS

finished size: about 3½in x 1¾in (9cm x 4.5cm)

2 3in (7.5cm) squares from a sheet of mediumweight one-sided red paper

Paper glue

1 To make the head: start with one square of paper, coloured side facing upward, in a diamond shape. Fold in half from bottom to top, unfold, then turn to make crease vertical.

2 Fold the two lower outer sloping edges inward to align with the vertical middle crease.

3 Fold the bottom point upward to touch the top horizontal edges of the flaps. Do not crease all the way across, but make a pinch mark where this line meets the vertical middle line. Unfold right back to Step 2.

4 Fold the corners of the flaps folded in Step 2 outward on a crease connecting the upper corners and the pinch mark made in Step 3.

5 Turn paper over and fold the top point downward on a crease connecting the upper corners at left and right.

6 Fold the right-hand outer sloping edge in to align with the vertical middle line.

7 Fold back by a small amount the upper inner corner at the top of the rectangular flap folded in Step 6 to create an eye. Fold the lower corner of this flap upward, extending the crease both sides to the outer edges to make the moustache.

8 To make the hat: start with the second square, white side facing upward. Fold in half, from bottom to top, unfold, then turn to a diamond shape with the crease as shown.

9 Fold the left point carefully to the right, where it meets the crease line from Step 8, making the new crease extend to the top point.

10 Unfold the flap from Step 9, then fold the upper right sloping edge across to the left to align with this crease.

11 Unfold Step 10, turn over so that the last creases are in a point at the top. Fold a small amount of paper inward at the top and at the bottom.

12 At the bottom, double the small triangle over itself three times until you have a long, thin border slightly extending beyond the middle creases.

13 Turn the paper over. Refold left and right flaps in turn, using existing creases made in steps 9–10. Tuck the lower corner of the second flap to be folded into the small white pocket of the trim of the first. Fold point of hat to one side.

14 Turn hat over and slide onto the head, using a touch of glue to keep in place. Glue onto a parcel, writing the person's name on the beard.

73

MATERIALS
(to make one star)

finished size: approximately 5½in (14cm) across

5 3in (7.5cm) squares of mediumweight gold or silver paper

1 Start with the square of paper, with the white side facing upward, in a diamond shape and fold in half from bottom to top. Unfold, turn paper around so that middle crease is vertical. Fold the two lower, sloping outer edges inward to meet the middle crease. This is a kite base.

2 Fold upper sloping edge at left across the model, so that the top point aligns with right-hand corner of kite, while the left-hand corner aligns with the middle crease.

3 Unfold, repeating Step 2 with upper right sloping edge. Unfold.

4 With left hand, hold model about halfway up right-hand edge. Allow upper section of flap to open out slightly, so that you can push in paper at top right-hand point.

5 Continue pushing top right-hand corner inward until it turns inside out. The crease crossing the right flap changes from a valley to a mountain (*see p. 12*) and the upper right-hand portion of the paper folds down on existing crease. Pinch to a point at right, flattening flap on creases.

6 Make sure that as the right-hand flap moves across, it tucks in behind the left-hand flap, as shown.

7 The finished unit should be slightly three dimensional with the creases arranged as shown. Repeat Steps 1–7 for the other units.

8 To assemble, hold the first unit in your left hand as in Step 7, but rotated through a 90° angle. The

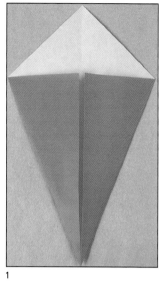

1

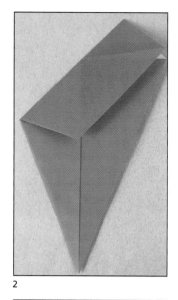

2

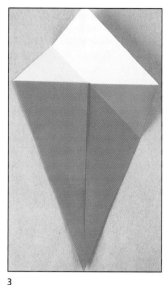

3

4

5

6

next one slides into the "pocket" formed in steps 4–6.

9 When the second unit is in place, there is a small triangular flap left above the raw edge at the middle of the first unit. Valley fold (*see p. 12*) downward, tucking it between the two layers of the front flap .

10 Join remaining units in the same way – the third unit slides into the second, the fourth into the third and the fifth into the fourth. Finally, join first unit to fifth to make the star symmetrical. Make other stars using the same method.

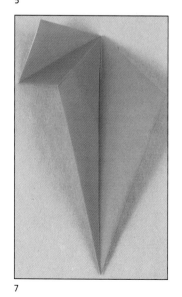

7

8

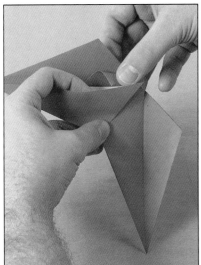

9

10

FIVE-POINTED STAR

Made from gold or silver paper, this star looks superb on top of the Christmas tree, or hanging with other stars. It was created by Nick Robinson of the UK and Tomoko Fuse of Japan. This model is a fine example of "modular origami" where several pieces of paper make the units, which are then joined by a folding technique. Use five 3in (7.5cm) paper squares for a medium star; just increase the square size for a larger one.

GIFTS

1

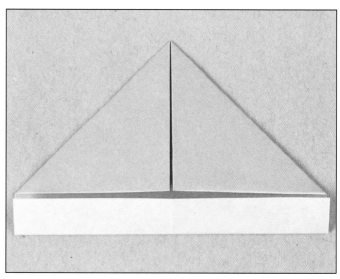

2

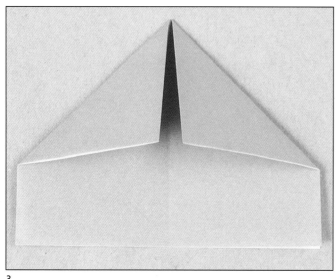

3

4

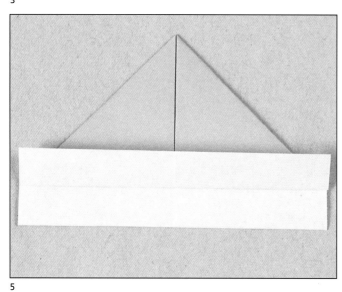

5

1 Start with the white side of the patterned gift-wrap paper facing upward, with the short sides of the rectangle in a horizontal position. First fold the paper in half, by taking the bottom edge up to meet the top edge and crease well.

2 Fold left-hand edge of the paper across to the right. Crease, unfold, and then rotate the paper around so that the folded edge formed in Step 1 now appears at top.

3 Fold the top left- and right-hand corners of the paper downward, so that they align exactly with the

middle vertical crease that was made earlier in Step 2.

4 Fold the bottom edge up, so that it lies along the lower edge of the two triangular flaps folded in Step 3. Turn the paper over and repeat this action on the other side, using the folded edge beneath as your guide.

5 Take the horizontal strip formed in Step 4 and fold it over once again. Turn the model over and repeat this fold on the other side to hold the hat together. Make other party hats in the same way.

CHILD'S PARTY HAT

MATERIALS

(to make one hat)

1 sheet of patterned gift-wrap paper, trimmed to size

This traditional design of hat is ideal to make if you are in a rush to organize a child's party, as the origami folds are so simple. You can even make a game out of it and get the children to make their own hats. They can then proudly take them home at the end of the party. Brightly patterned gift-wrap paper is the best to use and you will need to experiment with hat sizes by making some sample hats out of sheets of tabloid newspaper first. Generally, a sheet of gift-wrap paper is about right for an adult's head, so for children you will need to trim roughly about 1–2in (2.5–5cm) from adjacent sides of the rectangular sheet.

79

1 Start with the square of paper in a diamond shape. Fold in the points from top to bottom and side to side, unfolding each time. Then turn around to a square and insert book folds (see p. 12) in both vertical and horizontal directions. Turn to a diamond shape again and blintz fold (see p. 12) the four corners neatly into the middle, where the existing creases intersect.

2 Turn the paper over, arrange in a square, and blintz four corners to the middle as shown in Step 1.

3 Fold in half by bringing the bottom folded edge up to meet the top edge.

4 Hold the model with the fold made in Step 3 toward you, placing your fingers and thumbs a short distance from the vertical middle line. Push the outer corners inward, so that the upper corners meet in the middle and the fingers and thumbs at the bottom.

5 Holding firmly, carefully pull out each of the model's four flaps gathered around the closed point nearest to you, to form four small pockets. The model can also be turned upside down at this stage to make a salt cellar.

6 Place your fingers and thumbs up into the pockets, with your thumbs in the nearest pockets and your index fingers in the farthest. Operate the fortune teller by first parting your hands slightly, opening the model horizontally.

7 By parting your fingers away from your thumbs, you can also open the model vertically. Draw in your numbers and the resulting predictions on the fortune teller, and then open and close the model as detailed to the first number that is chosen by the player.

1

2

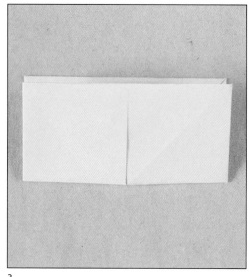

3

4

5

6

EASY LEVEL

FORTUNE TELLER

This popular puzzle is fun for everyone to make, and it keeps children amused for hours. A normal 6in (15cm) paper square makes a handy model; just increase the square's size for a bigger one. To use the puzzle, number the inner panels one to eight. You then open and close the model in alternate directions according to the chosen number. Now ask for another number from a displayed flap. The flap is then opened to reveal that person's fortune.

MATERIALS
finished size: 2½in x 2½in (6.5cm x 6.5cm)

1 6in (15cm) square
from a sheet of lightweight,
dual-coloured pale paper

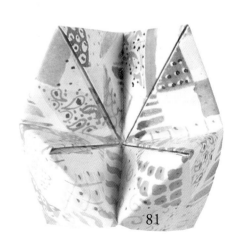

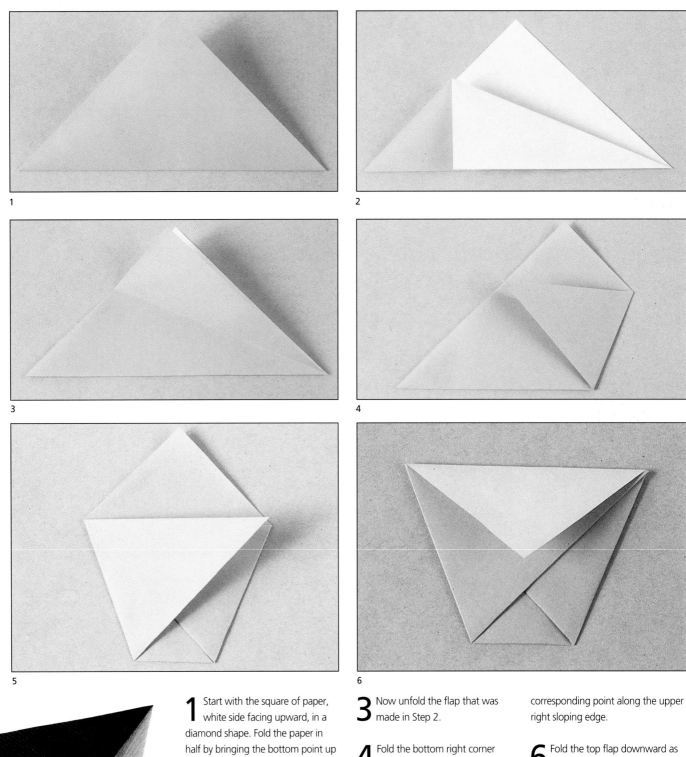

1
2
3
4
5
6

1 Start with the square of paper, white side facing upward, in a diamond shape. Fold the paper in half by bringing the bottom point up to meet the top.

2 Fold upper right sloping edge of top flap downward, so that it now aligns with the folded edge at the bottom of this triangular shape.

3 Now unfold the flap that was made in Step 2.

4 Fold the bottom right corner across to the left to touch the end of the crease made in Step 2.

5 You now need to fold the bottom left point across to the right, so that it meets up with the

corresponding point along the upper right sloping edge.

6 Fold the top flap downward as far as it will go. Turn the model over and repeat behind. Bear in mind that the cup will not stand on its own, and when filled will need to lean against an object. Make other cups using the same method.

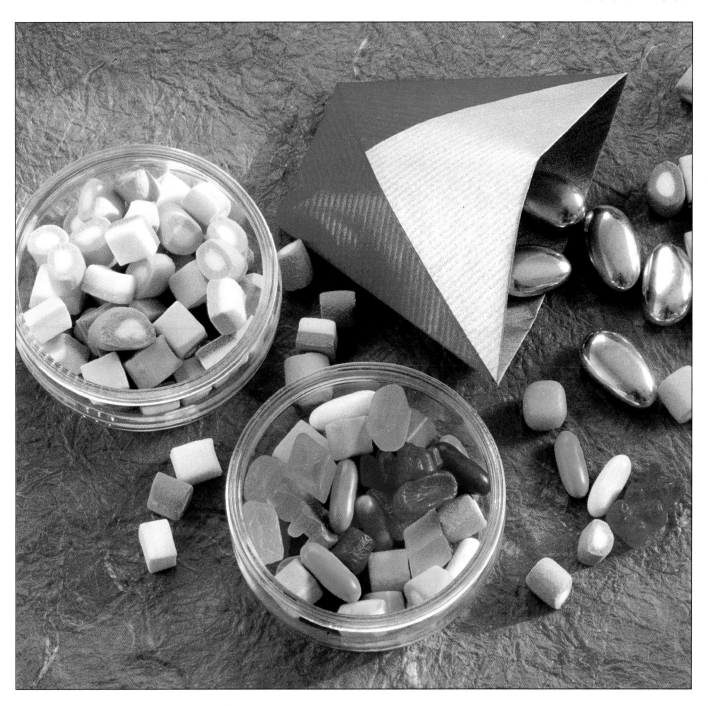

GOODY CUP

This versatile paper cup is made from a traditional origami design and has several different uses. You can fill it with sweets and other small presents for children to take home as a party bag from a birthday celebration, it can hold some savouries, or you can even use it as a drinking cup.

The folds are simple to make and it is easy to model several cups for a child's party in an evening. If you want to make a cup to drink from, always use a 6in (15cm) square of glossy or foil paper. But take care when the cups have liquid in them as they will not stand up on their own.

MATERIALS

(to make one cup)

finished size: about 3¾in x 3½in (9.5cm x 9cm)

1 8in (20cm) square from a mediumweight sheet of two-sided coloured paper

83

WINDMILL TOY

Young children will love to take this toy with them when they go out for walks as the windmills will spin around in the breeze. The toy can also make an attractive decoration for the house. You can make several windmills together and place them in a colourful bucket filled with sand in a prominent corner in the hall or living room.

This traditional model is, in fact, an origami base itself. It is part of a folding exercise called the Multiform, where the paper is manipulated step-by-step to make a different model each time. Make the two sizes of windmill in brightly coloured or patterned paper and safely attach them with plastic clips to thin green sticks.

MATERIALS

(to make one windmill)

finished size – big windmill: 9in x 9in (23.5cm x 23.5cm), small windmill: 6½in x 6½in (17cm x 17cm)

1 9½in (24cm) square from a sheet of mediumweight brightly coloured or patterned paper

1 7in (17.5cm) square from a different sheet of mediumweight brightly coloured or patterned paper

Craft knife

Plastic clips for paddy bags, cut in half, or other two-part plastic clips

Strong glue or transparent adhesive tape

Thin green sticks (from garden centres)

1

2

3

4

5

6

1 Start with the larger square of paper, white side facing upward in a diamond shape. Fold the paper in half from bottom to top and side to side, folding and unfolding each time. Turn to a square and fold in the two book folds (*see p. 12*), folding and unfolding the paper.

2 Fold the bottom right sloping edge inward to align with the middle crease. Repeat with top left sloping edge. Unfold. Fold the remaining opposite, sloping edges inward to middle line. Again, unfold to give the necessary crease pattern.

3 Take hold of the right corner and pinch two adjacent outer edges together on the diagonal valley crease (*see p. 12*). Start to collapse the paper also using the adjacent creases made in Step 2.

4 Continue to pinch the paper into the middle, pushing it down.

5 Then press down flat to the right, completing the collapse.

6 Repeat steps 3–5 with the remaining three corners of the square, working clockwise, remembering that with subsequent corners at least one flap from Step 2 will be folded in position. Take the smaller square of coloured paper and make the second windmill using the above method. To fix the windmills to the green stick, put the small windmill on top of the big one and make a small hole through both of them with the craft knife. Put one end of the plastic clip though the hole and clip the other end onto the other side. Use strong glue on the clip at the back of the windmills and the green stick and hold together to fix firmly in place. Alternatively, use small pieces of adhesive tape to attach the plastic back of the clip to the stick. Make other windmills in the same way.

1

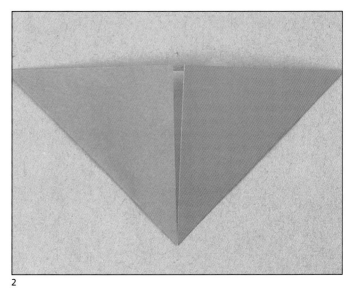

2

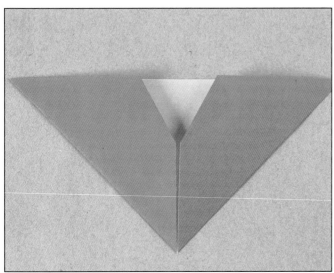

3

4

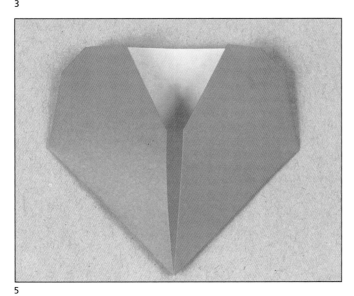

5

1 Start with the rectangle of red paper, coloured side facing downward, with the short sides horizontal. Fold paper in half by bringing bottom edge up to meet the top edge. Unfold, and turn the paper around so the crease is vertical.

2 Fold the bottom left- and right-hand corners inward to align with the vertical middle crease.

3 Mountain fold (*see p. 12*) the tips of the flaps folded in Step 2 behind to create the cleft in the heart. The angle and amount is not too important, see next steps.

4 Turn model over, then fold the outer corners inward to touch the vertical middle crease, a short distance down from the top edge.

5 Turn over once more and shape the heart further by mountain folding a small amount of each upper corner behind. Fold the A4 piece of card in half from left to right and place the heart on the front. Glue in position. Take the white or cream rectangle and fold in bottom outer corners to make an arrow shape. Write a special message on it with the metallic pen and insert in the heart to finish the card.

VALENTINE'S CARD

Everybody loves receiving a romantic card on Valentine's Day and what better way of showing someone you care about them than to make them a special card with a red heart on the front.

A small tapered card can be inserted in the top of the heart so that you can write a special message to your loved one. Write this with a gold metallic pen to add that special touch to the card.

The heart, designed by the author, is made from a small rectangle (a square cut in half makes two models). In the project a medium-sized heart is detailed that will fit on an A5-sized folded card.

If you want to make a larger red heart, as shown above, just increase the size proportionately of the rectangle that you begin with. The red paper used for the heart doesn't have to be double-sided as you fold the model in such a way that the white will be hidden and only the red side will show when the heart is complete.

The folds that you make in steps 3–5 are fairly arbitrary, the exact shaping to create the finished heart relies on your own personal folding technique.

MATERIALS

finished size of heart: about 2¾in x 3¼in (7cm x 8.5cm); message card: 3¾in x 2¼in (9.5cm x 5.5cm)

1 3in x 5¾in (7.5cm x 14cm) rectangle from a sheet of mediumweight red paper

1 3¾in x 2¼in (9.5cm x 5.5cm) rectangle from a sheet of mediumweight white or cream card

1 A4-sized rectangle cut from a sheet of white or cream card

Paper glue

Gold metallic pen

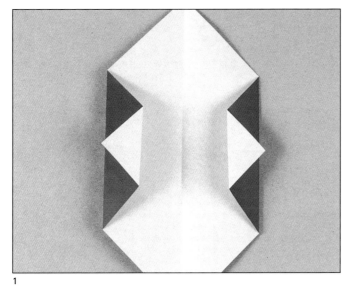

1

2

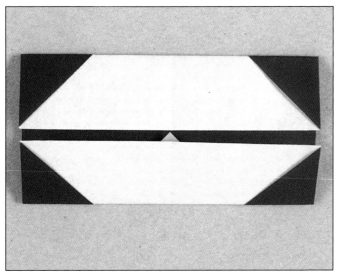

3

4

MATERIALS

finished size: about 3in x 6¼in (7.5cm x 15.5cm)

1 9in (22.5cm) square
from a sheet of mediumweight
brown or black paper

1 For coloured corners on the blotter, start with the square of paper, white side facing upward, in a diamond shape. Fold the paper in half by taking the bottom point up to meet the top and from side to side, folding and unfolding each time. Then bring left- and right-hand points to the middle of the paper and fold each back on itself to align with outer folded edge, as shown.

2 Turn the paper over from right to left, keeping it the same way up. Fold the top and bottom points inward to align with the middle line of the model.

3 Fold the upper and lower outer folded edges in to align with the horizontal middle line. The blotter is now complete and a sheet of blotting paper can be placed inside it under the corners.

4 If you want to make the desk blotter into a picture frame, turn the model over, keeping it horizontal. Lift up the two triangular flaps that were folded in Step 1 to 90° to the rest of the model. Turn the frame over again and the picture frame will stand up. Don't forget to trim down any photographs that you want to place in the frame.

EASY LEVEL

DESK BLOTTER

If you still like writing personal letters to family and friends with your own fountain pen, then having an ink blotter on your desk in your study at home will prove extremely useful.

If you don't have need of a blotter, you can just follow Step 4 and change the model into a landscape picture frame instead. As diagonal creases are necessary in this variation, the finished frame will be quite narrow, so you'll need to trim down any

photographs that you want to display in it to the right size. Make the blotter or frame out of one-sided, mediumweight, good-quality black or brown paper so that it blends well with your photographs or chosen blotting paper.

When making the model, start with the white side of the paper facing upward if you want to have coloured corners; for white corners, just start with the coloured side facing upward.

The picture frame model is the author's adaptation of a traditional origami design. With the changes to the folds, triangular flaps appear at the back of the model, which can then be opened out to make a proper stand for the frame.

To assemble the fish mobile, cut one wood stick to 8in (20.5cm), one to 11¾in (29.5cm) and two more to 4in (10cm) long. Cut a piece of thread about 12in (30cm) and tie to middle of 8in (20.5cm) section and then onto middle of 11¾in (29.5cm) section and leave hanging. Attach 2¼in (6cm) threads to each end of the first section and hang a fish either end by taping thread to each one's back. Tie 4¼in (11cm) threads to each end of the second section and attach to middle of both 4in (10cm) sections. Then tie 3in (7.5cm) threads to either ends of these sections and tape to back of a fish to make four fish on the two sections. Tie two 2in (5cm) threads either side of the middle of the 11¾in (29.5cm) section and tape two more fish in position. Finally, tape the last (ninth) fish to the long thread still hanging from the middle. Adjust threads to balance mobile. Attach a hook to top thread and hang from ceiling hook.

FISH MOBILE

Mobiles are always popular with young children, and they will love watching this one moving in the breeze with its cheeky fish models. Place near a door, window or close to a fan so that the mobile gets enough air movement.

The three fish are designed by the author, who experimented with various folds to achieve the different shapes. Make the Goldfish and the Blue Fish out of marbled paper, so that you get the real effect of the fish scales. The Stripy Fish looks best in a black and white striped paper to resemble a tropical fish, but you can use another colour combination if you prefer. Nine fish feature in the mobile, so make three of each type.

If you don't want to make a mobile, the fish could be included in a sea mural in a bedroom or bathroom.

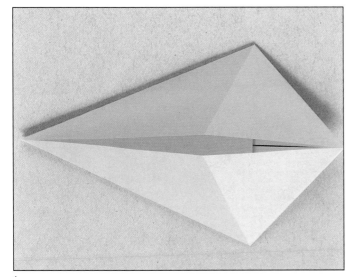

1

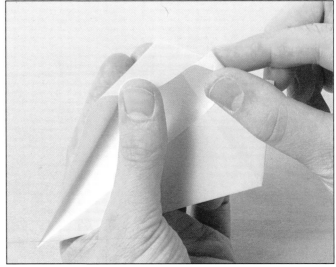

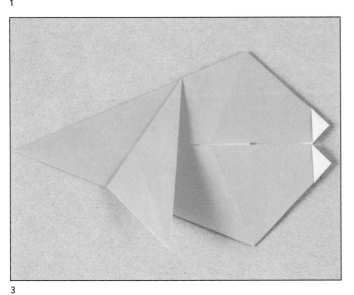

2

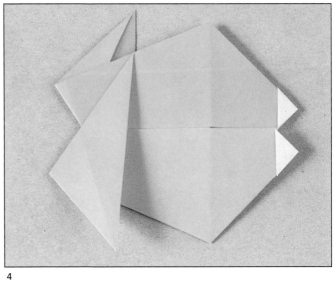

3

4

BLUE FISH

This fish is very simple to make, once you've mastered the folds necessary in the initial Fish Base (*see p. 15*). It is this base which gives you the fish's outline shape.

Fold carefully when you are making the fish's "nose" so that both the top and bottom triangular tips are even and that they line up equally.

Remember to crease the fish's tail accurately in Step 4, so that you achieve the necessary sharp angles.

MATERIALS
(to make one fish)

finished size: about 3¼in x 3¾in (8.5cm x 9.5cm)

1 5¾in (14.5cm) square from a sheet of mediumweight blue marbled paper

1 Start with the Fish Base (*see p. 15*). Place the fish horizontally with the wider point to the right.

2 Lift up top raw edge that runs horizontally across the model, opening out the pocket at the front of the head. Turn the tip of the upper right-hand flap back on itself by a small amount, then flatten the paper once more. Repeat with lower portion of model.

3 Fold top point at left downward on a sloping crease to form half of tail as shown. The amount of paper folded isn't too important, but the front edge of the tail in this new position should be vertical.

4 Turn model over and fold the point at the right upward on a sloping crease. Both front edges of each half of the tail should line up in a straight line. Make the other two fish using the same method.

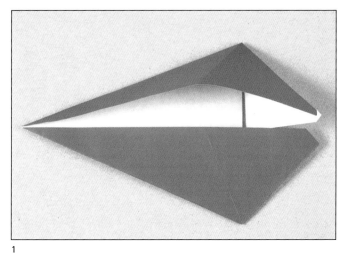

1

2

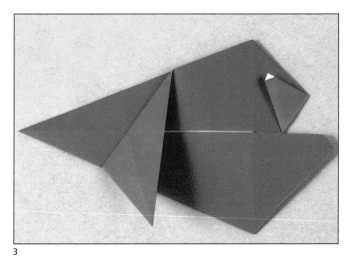

3

4

EASY LEVEL

STRIPY FISH

Similar in style to the Blue Fish that is detailed on page 91, this stripy fish is also made from the Fish Base (*see p. 15*), but by altering some of the folds it is given other features so that it particularly resembles a tropical fish.

By folding the front of the upper and lower right-hand flaps in a slightly different way, you can make the fish look as though it is swimming along and feeding with its mouth open.

It is important when you make this fish to fold both the top and lower part of the tail neatly and precisely, so that it stands out when hanging in the mobile.

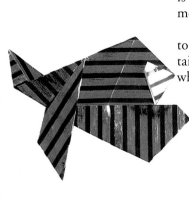

MATERIALS
(to make one fish)
finished size: about 3½in x 3½in (9cm x 9cm)
1 5¾in (14.5cm) square from a sheet of mediumweight black and white striped paper

1 Start with the Fish Base (*see p. 15*). Place the fish horizontally with the wider point to the right. Start to lift up the top flap.

2 Repeat Step 2 of the Blue Fish on the upper right flap, but then fold the tip over by a slightly less amount. At the bottom, the tip is doubled over twice, but this time it is folded inside (so no white shows on the outside). Then fold the upper right flap back across to the left on a

sloping crease, to position the eye (the tiny white triangle) as desired.

3 Fold the upper left point down as in Step 3 of the Blue Fish.

4 Turn the model over so that the tail is at the right and the eye is still at the top of the upper left portion. Fold up both layers of the lower long edge, the sloping crease begins a short distance from the bottom corner and cuts right across the flap of the tail beneath. Fold the lower tail portion back down into position by making a small squash fold (*see p. 13*). Then push down the triangular flap so that it helps to give shape to the lower tail flap. Turn the model over. Make the other two fish using the same method.

MATERIALS
(to make one fish)

finished size: about 1½in x 4¾in (3cm x 12cm)

1 5¾in (14.5cm) square from a sheet of mediumweight red marbled paper

1 Start with the Fish Base (*see p. 15*). Place fish horizontally with wider point to the right. Repeat Step 2 of Blue Fish on lower-right flap, but fold tip over twice.

2 Hold model in left hand about halfway in from left. Lift up upper horizontal raw edge at right, again hollowing out the pocket at the front. The upper flap's tip is now swivelled across toward the tail to align with the horizontal middle line. Also, pinch in a diagonal valley crease (*see p. 12*) between the top corner and the horizontal middle line.

3 Squash down flat to form a square shape.

4 Fold model in half, from bottom to top, on the middle crease.

5 Turn over and fold left corner of upper horizontal flap downward. The amount is not too important, but the crease should extend to upper right corner to form the fin.

6 At the right there are two flaps. Open the outer layer slightly, take hold of inner point and valley fold it outward on a sloping crease to form tail. Flatten model as before.

7 Double tail again, so that valley crease runs along the paper's inner thickness. Turn over. Make other two fish using the same method.

INTERMEDIATE LEVEL

GOLDFISH

The folding in this fish takes more skill than the first two, so experiment with them first before attempting to make this one. Again start with the Fish Base (*see p.15*), but take time to fold steps 3 and 4, because if you rush the folding you won't achieve the neat square that is necessary for this fish shape.

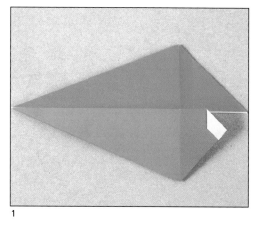

1

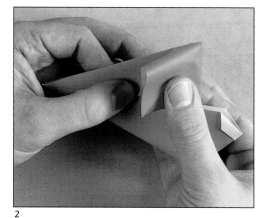

2

3

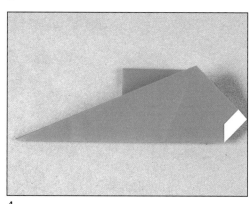

4

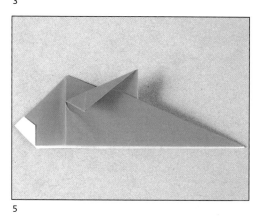

5

6

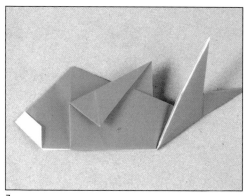

7

INTERMEDIATE LEVEL

BASKET

Fill up this basket with some fruit or nuts and give it to a friend as a special present that you have made yourself.

This model is designed by Koya Ohashi and in origami terms is called "climactic", which means that it does not come to life until the final step when the model is opened out or turned inside out. The Preliminary Base (*see p. 14*) and the first two steps from Party Sailboat (*see p. 24*) are used for the basket's first folds.

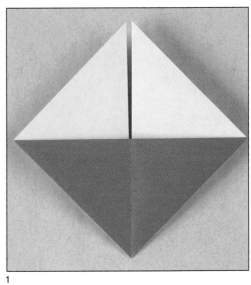

1

MATERIALS

finished size: the basket has a base of about 4¾in (12cm)

1 12in (30cm) square from a sheet of mediumweight brown or beige two-sided paper

1 Start by folding the Preliminary Base with the square, coloured side facing upward, and the closed point at the bottom (*see p. 14*) then make follow step 1–2 of the Party Sailboat (*see p. 24*).

2 Fold the top flap at the right across to the left using the vertical middle crease as an axis. Turn the paper over and repeat this fold behind.

3 On the top flap only, fold the upper right sloping edge inward, so that it aligns with the vertical middle crease.

4 Repeat Step 3 using the left-hand flap.

5 Turn the model over, from right to left. Now fold a very small amount of paper downward at the top, making sure that you fold the upper layer and the spiky point underneath as one.

6 Fold the edge at the top over itself once again.

7 Fold it over once again, so that you join the two halves of the handle together.

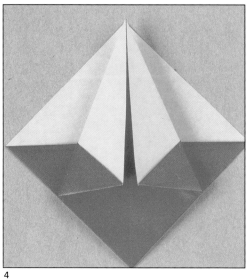

2

3

4

5

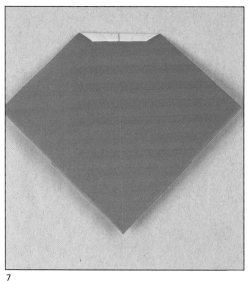

6

7

8 Fold the outer sloping edges at the top inward to align with the vertical middle crease, repeating steps 3–4.

9 Place your thumb inside one of the triangular-shaped pockets about halfway up the model. Hollow it out, then, pushing upward and outward against the horizontal folded edge at the bottom, swivel this pocket outward. Keep doing this until the horizontal crease aligns with the outer sloping edge of the handle.

10 Repeat this folding with the three remaining pockets.

11 To establish the base creases, fold the bottom point upward on a crease connecting the left and right lower corners. Crease firmly.

12 Unfold the bottom flap of the model once more.

13 Then carefully separating the two halves of the handle, hollow out the basket completely and pinch well to shape the base creases.

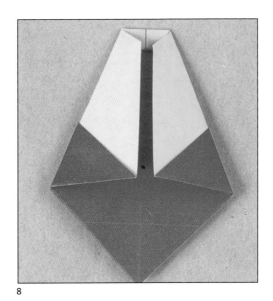

8

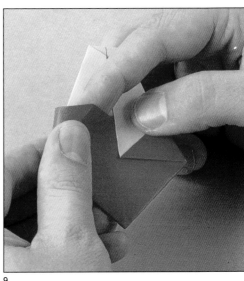

9

10

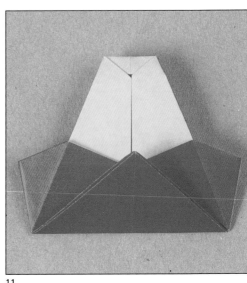

11

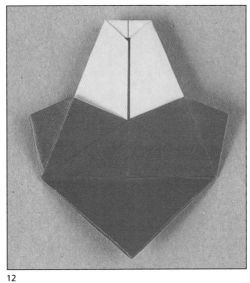

12

13

DESK TIDIES

Keeping track of all your pens and pencils or the children's crayons at home is always difficult, but by making this desk tidy out of eye-catching paper you can store them away neatly. If you want to have a matching set of tidies, make the long version as well and store some small envelopes, notelets or note books in it.

Designed by Giuseppe Baggi of Italy, the desk tidy's sequence of folds needs to be followed systematically to achieve the correct crease pattern. Always leave the paper the correct way up and with the right side facing you, so that you get the right creases at Step 11 when you have to collapse the box into shape. If you want to make bigger desk tidies than detailed, just increase the paper size proportionately.

MATERIALS

finished size of upright version: 3in x 2¼in x 3in (7.5cm x 5.5cm x 7.5cm) long version: 2¼in x 7½in x 2¼in (5.5cm x 19cm x 5.5cm)

1 A4-sized rectangle cut from a heavyweight sheet of fleck or marbled or similar two-sided paper

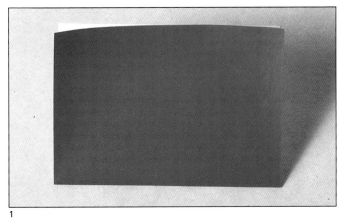

1

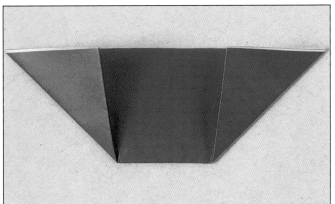

2

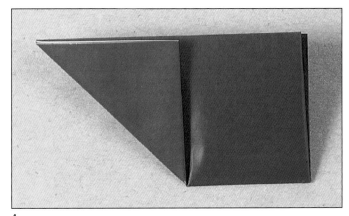

3

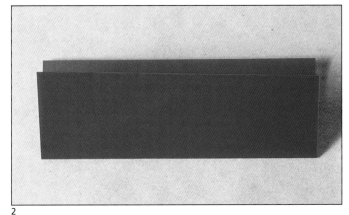

4

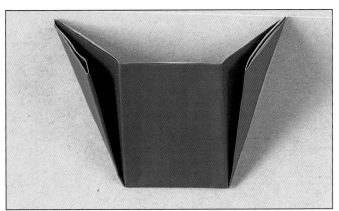

5

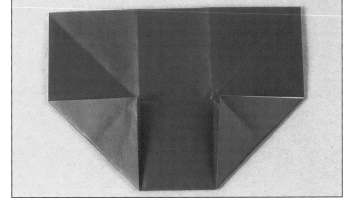

6

1 Start with the rectangle white side facing upward and the short sides of the paper running horizontally. Fold the paper in half, bringing the bottom edge right up to meet the top edge. If you want to create a long, shallow tidy (*as shown in the picture on p. 97*), start instead with the long sides of the paper horizontal, but fold the tidy in exactly the same way.

2 Fold the new lower edge up to meet the top edge.

3 Fold the two outer vertical edges inward on a diagonal sloping crease, so that they align with the top edge.

4 Mountain fold (*see p. 12*) the right-hand point behind, creating a vertical crease that runs

along the edge of the triangular flap made in Step 3.

5 Unfold and repeat on the left-hand side.

6 Unfold model back to Step 1, making sure that the only fold made runs along the bottom and the horizontal crease at the middle is now a valley crease (*see p. 12*). Bring

the outer corners at the bottom inward on a sloping crease to align with this middle horizontal line.

7 Repeat at the top, bringing only the top layer down, leaving the back flap unfolded.

8 Fold the upper portion of the top layer of paper downward, using the horizontal middle crease.

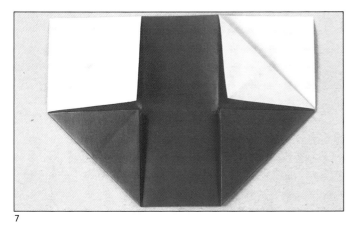

7

8

9

10

11

12

9 Hold the model right in the middle of the upper flap with your left hand, and then gently start to pull the middle panel of the lower section upward, until it is at a 90° angle to the upper flap. By doing this, the left- and right-hand sides of the desk tidy will start to fold inward automatically on the creases that have already been made in the previous steps.

10 Pinch the dimensions of the tidy into a more rigid shape, making sure that you reinforce the creases well.

11 At the open end of the tidy there are three important creases: a sloping crease from the outer right-hand corner to the lower inner corner; a similar crease at the left and a horizontal crease connecting the two. Using all three creases as valley folds, collapse the paper bringing the final side of the tidy into position and leaving two triangular flaps that project out from the corners.

12 Fold these flaps back toward you, so that they lie along the long sides of the tidy. Then tuck the corners of the triangular flaps inside the pockets under the diagonal sloping folded edges that run down each of the sides. Go all around the tidy and pinch the outer creases firmly into the right shape.

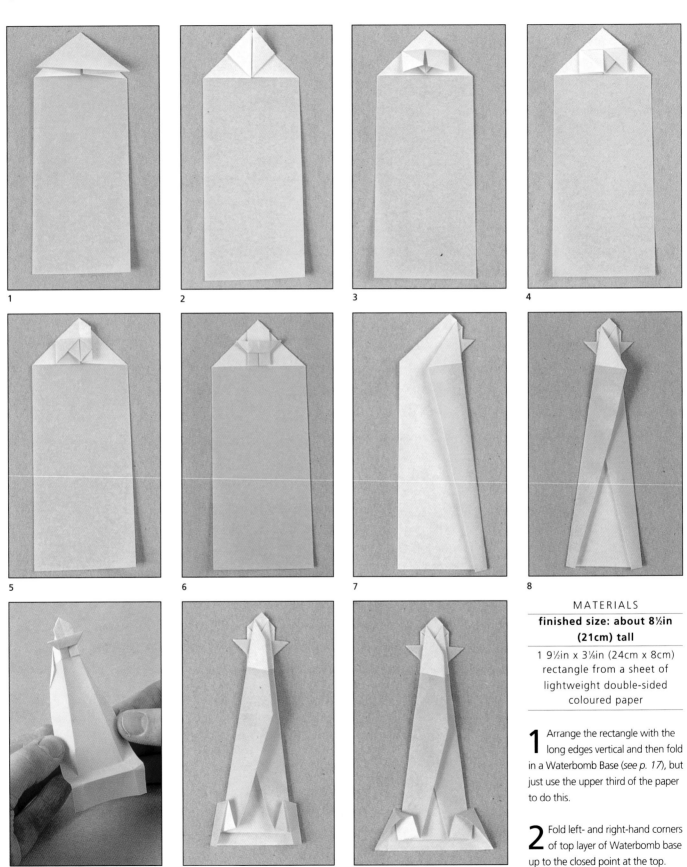

1

2

3

4

5

6

7

8

9

10

11

MATERIALS

finished size: about 8½in (21cm) tall

1 9½in x 3⅛in (24cm x 8cm) rectangle from a sheet of lightweight double-sided coloured paper

1 Arrange the rectangle with the long edges vertical and then fold in a Waterbomb Base (*see p. 17*), but just use the upper third of the paper to do this.

2 Fold left- and right-hand corners of top layer of Waterbomb base up to the closed point at the top.

3 Using creases made in Step 2, squash fold (*see p. 13*) both flaps to form two small squares.

4 Fold inner corner of right square outward, folding in half diagonally. Repeat on left-hand side.

5 Mountain fold (*see p. 12*) outer edges of middle section and right-hand square behind to meet middle crease. Repeat on left.

6 Open out left- and right-hand flaps either side of vertical middle slit, pushing out and down until they lie flat to rear flaps of the Waterbomb Base. The middle point will open out and squash upward, flattening into the "balcony" shown.

7 Turn model over and fold right edge across to left on a crease that crosses through lower edge of balcony, getting wider toward the bottom. This crease can be adjusted, with practice, to get the right shape.

8 Repeat Step 7 on the left. Mountain fold projecting point at right behind.

9 Take care with this tricky step. Turn model over and hold firmly. Open out bottom left and right flaps at the back. Next, fold bottom edge upward by a small amount, then back down on itself to give a pleat. The second fold should bring the raw bottom edge down beyond the folded edge. Finally, re-fold side flaps, pressing all layers flat, as shown. Turn over.

10 Open out two small flaps at the bottom until they lie flat to the working surface.

11 Make two small squash folds so that new creases slope outward from lighthouse base to lower corners – the lighthouse's rock. Turn completed model over.

INTERMEDIATE LEVEL

LIGHTHOUSE BOOKMARK

You will never lose your position in the latest novel that you are reading with this stylish bookmark. Alternatively, you can use it to mark the current day or week in your home or office diary.

This traditional bookmark design originated in China, where it first appeared in Maying Soong's 1948 book, *The Art of Chinese Paperfolding for Young and Old*. Make the model out of a fairly thin, crisp double-sided coloured paper, and follow all the steps carefully, especially when forming the top of the lighthouse, as it is easy to make a mistake. The creases that need to be made in steps 7–8 are fairly arbitrary, depending on the desired width of the lighthouse – they should taper gradually at the top.

G I F T S

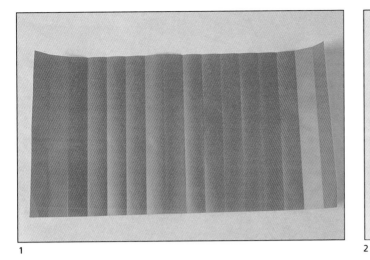

1

2

3

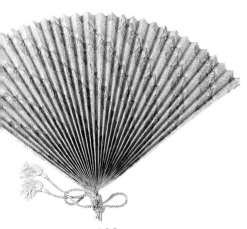

4

MATERIALS

finished size: about 22in x 44in (55cm x 110cm) when opened out

2 large rectangles of Japanese *washi* paper or patterned mediumweight paper

Double-sided adhesive tape

Wired ribbon

1 Start with the first patterned rectangle of paper, patterned side facing upward. Start by dividing the paper into 16 equal vertical sections. Using valley creases (*see p. 12*), first fold the paper in half, short edge to short edge. Unfold. Then fold the two short edges inward to align with the middle crease. Unfold. Next, fold each of the short edges, first to the creases just made, then across the model to the same crease on the opposite side. Fold and unfold each time. The paper is now divided into eight equal vertical sections. Keeping the paper the same way up, place creases in between the vertical creases by folding each outer edge inward to align with the next vertical crease, then with every alternative vertical valley crease. Fold and unfold

each time until you have divided the paper into 16 equal vertical sections, as shown above.

2 Turn the paper over. Now place vertical valley creases in between the existing creases. This can be achieved by folding each of the short edges in turn, first to align with the nearest mountain crease (*see p. 12*), then to each subsequent mountain crease, folding and unfolding the paper each time. When finished the paper will be divided into 32 equal vertical sections.

3 Turn the paper back over. Now you need to collapse the fan model using all the existing creases made in their alternate valley and mountain directions.

4 Hold the completed fan at the bottom and allow it to spread open. Make the second fan with the second patterned rectangle using the same method as described above. When both fans are finished, spread them open and join them together with pieces of double-side adhesive tape at the back. Then wrap some wired ribbon around the base of the fan and tie in a bow or leave ends loose. Hang the fan on the wall or display in front of an unused fireplace.

DECORATIVE FAN

Make an eye-catching feature out of an unused fireplace in the summer, or create a stunning wall hanging in an oriental-style bedroom or living room with this delightful paper fan.

You can make it from a large rectangle of Japanese *washi* paper, as shown here, which is richly coloured and quite waxy to the touch. This type of paper holds a "soft" crease that is ideal for the fan's delicate appearance. Alternatively, you can choose a mediumweight, subtly patterned paper that is strong enough to hold the creases well, but will not tear too easily.

The process of making this traditional design of fan is called pleating, where you mathematically divide the paper into several equal vertical sections. The accuracy of the pleating is crucial in this project, so follow all the instructions precisely and take your time, making sure that each crease is where it should be before you finally flatten out the paper.

Do not worry too much about the exact proportions of the fan after it is finished, as it is very easy to trim a little off the top or bottom when it is folded, just using a sharp craft knife.

Fold the fan from two large rectangles of paper, as one rectangle is not big enough to display or hang on its own, so you need to make two, then join them both together with tape so that they open out into one really spectacular fan that everyone will notice and admire.

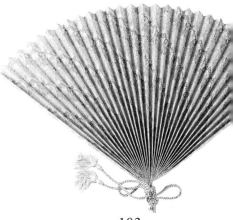

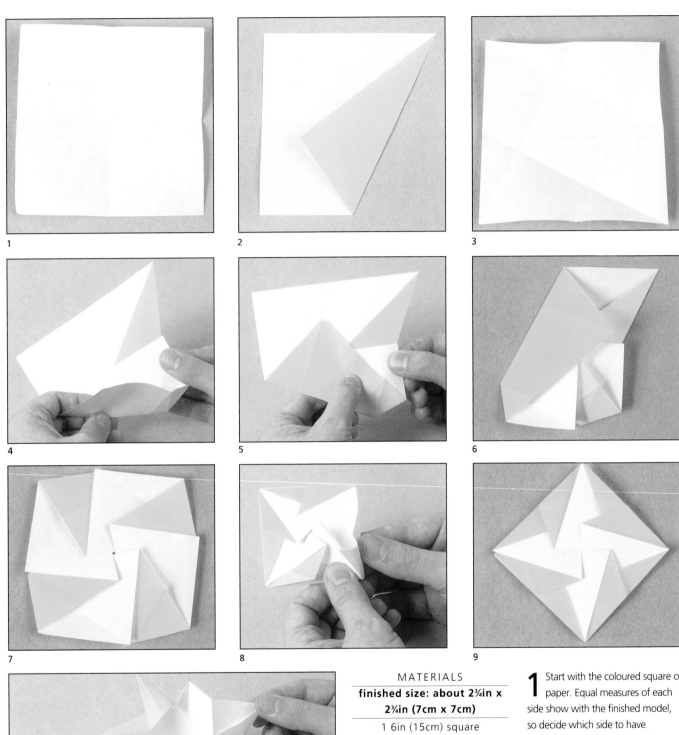

1

2

3

4

5

6

7

8

9

10

MATERIALS

finished size: about 2¾in x 2¾in (7cm x 7cm)

1 6in (15cm) square from a sheet of mediumweight two-sided (duo) or one-sided coloured paper

1 Start with the coloured square of paper. Equal measures of each side show with the finished model, so decide which side to have uppermost. Fold in vertical and horizontal book folds (*see p. 12*), unfolding and folding each time.

2 Fold the lower right-hand corner across the paper, making a crease from the top right-hand corner to where the vertical book fold from Step 1 touches the lower edge. This is quite tricky to fold, so do it carefully.

3 Unfold flap, then, turning the paper around each time, repeat Step 2 with remaining corners. Unfold each time to give the crease pattern as shown.

4 Using the existing crease, re-fold the bottom right-hand corner. Then fold this point back on itself toward the right to align with the diagonal fold just made. A new crease forms beginning at the lower corner of the middle diamond shape, made in Step 3, crossing the top layer up to its raw edge. Start to lift up the left-hand side of the paper.

5 Squash the left-hand side of the paper down flat using the existing creases as shown.

6 Working in a clockwise direction, repeat steps 4–5 with the next corner.

7 Repeat steps 4–5 with the last two corners, making sure that with the last one, you lift out the folded edges of the first flap so that it can slip underneath in a neat, symmetrical pattern.

8 There are now four triangular flaps around a diamond shape in the middle. Using the diamond's creases, push the outer corner of one flap inward, so that you turn it inside out, then slowly collapse the model flat.

9 Repeat Step 8 with the other three corners.

10 To open the purse, take hold of any two opposite, pointed flaps and pull gently apart to put something inside. If your creases are sharp and accurate they will collapse back flat.

JAPANESE PURSE

Children, in particular, will be delighted when they receive some birthday or Christmas money hidden in the folds of this intricate purse. The purse can be tucked in their Christmas stockings along with their other small presents.

The purse is a traditional origami design and it is made with a symmetrical network of creases that collapse flat to form an attractive pattern. Work through the step-by-step instructions slowly, as the folding process is quite tricky to get right first time. The magic is in the last step where you can pull the completed purse apart, place paper money, stamps, small photographs or another small item inside, before folding it flat again. The purse can then be wrapped and posted to someone.

Use a two-coloured (duo) square to make a brightly coloured purse or a one-sided coloured square, so that some of the white reverse side shows, if preferred. The finished purse is about a quarter of the size of the starting square.

4 Fold lower left-hand sloping edge inward and across to meet opposite crease. Again only crease from bottom up to horizontal line.

5 Unfold and repeat with other three edges. Hold paper with left hand, and with right hand pinch right corner, emphasizing mountain crease (*see p. 12*) on horizontal. Repeat at left side, flexing diamond into shape.

6 Holding the left- and right-hand corners, push inward toward the middle vertical line. The folds of the diamond pattern collapse as the top of the paper is mountain folded behind on horizontal crease.

7 Press the paper flat to create a dart shape.

8 Fold top layer of outer sloping right-hand edge in to meet the vertical middle line. Hollow out pocket at top of model and squash the fold flat (*see p. 13*), so that upper point aligns with far edge of middle section.

9 Repeat this movement on the left-hand side.

ADVANCED LEVEL

HEART STICK PIN

Treat your loved one to an unusual present on Valentine's Day by making this heart stick pin that can be worn in the buttonhole of a jacket.

The stick pin, designed by Daniel Stillman, is quite difficult to make, so it is best to practise first on a larger 6in (15cm) square of scrap paper before you try to make it in the smaller size.

The model also needs a large amount of pre-creasing before you can collapse it to form the heart shape. Use some thin paper that is red on one side, and take care to fold extremely accurately so that you successfully complete the difficult steps 1–7.

MATERIALS

finished size about: 4¼in x 3¼in (11cm x 8.5cm)

1 3in (7.5cm) square
from a lightweight sheet of
one-sided red paper

1 Start with the square of paper, white side facing upward, in a diamond shape. Fold in crease lines by folding the bottom point up to meet the top and from side to side.

2 Fold lower right-hand sloping edge inward to meet vertical middle line, creasing only from the corner to meet horizontal line.

3 Unfold and, turning the paper around, repeat Step 2 with remaining edges. Turn paper over.

10 Fold top two middle flaps outward to meet mountain crease as shown. Fold underneath flaps outward slightly to form heart's clef. Shape heart with two valley folds (*see p. 12*) at each outer corner.

11 Fold the top layer, the pin, upward on the crease connecting the lower part of top coloured flaps. Fold pin back down on itself, creating a pleat. Fold bottom point of heart up inside model as far as it will go.

12 Narrow the pin by folding outer edges inward to meet middle line, making two squash folds at top. Valley fold lower corners of heart inward to meet middle line, shaping heart. Turn over to finish.

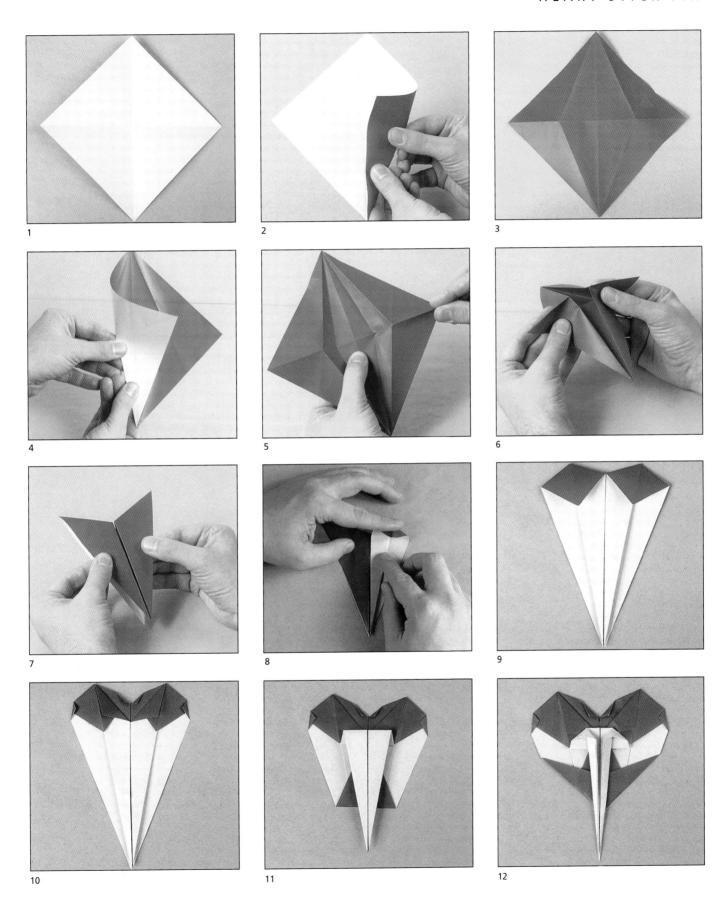

1

2

3

4

5

6

7

8

9

10

11

12

FLOWER CARD

This delicate floral design works so well when made with the origami technique, and looks stunning placed on a greetings card.

The flower was created by Yoshihide Momotani and is in the neat, simple origami style that is found throughout Japan. You can use different coloured papers to make the flower bud, calyx and leaves, or use a special origami paper (as shown) that is patterned by an airbrushing technique to varying degrees of one colour such as green, for example. Position the flower pieces on the card so that the design just "suggests" the stem. The flower and leaves are made from small pieces of paper, so try them out first on larger scrap paper until you are proficient with the folding.

MATERIALS

Flower bud: 1 3in (7.5cm) square from a sheet of lightweight pink paper

Calyx: 1 1½in (3cm) square from a sheet of lightweight green paper

Leaves: 5¾in (2cm) squares from a sheet of lightweight green paper

1 A4-sized rectangle cut from a sheet of white or cream card

Paper glue

1 To make flower bud: start with pink square of paper, coloured side facing upward. Book fold (*see p. 12*) paper in half both ways, folding and unfolding each time.

2 Turn paper over and arrange in diamond shape. Fold bottom point up to top, but make horizontal

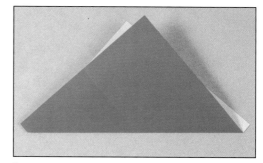

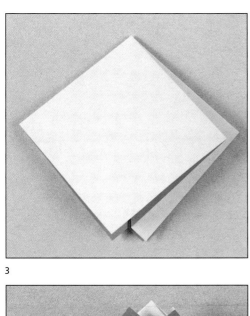

3

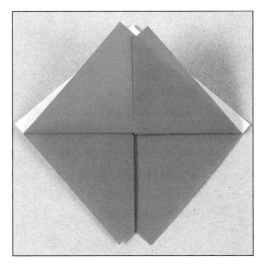

4

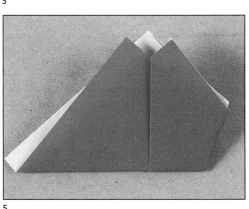

5

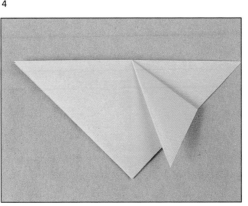

6

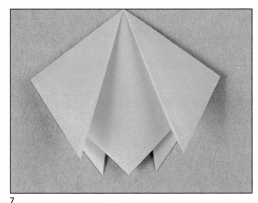

7

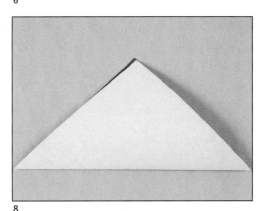

8

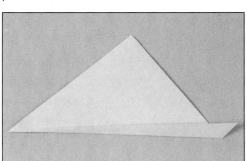

9

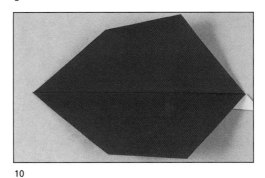

10

crease slightly off-centre, so that top flap lies slightly to the right, as shown. Fold carefully as the crease must intersect creases from Step 1.

3 Unfold Step 2, and using existing creases, collapse paper as in the Preliminary Base (*see p. 14*). Arrange with closed point at the top.

4 Fold both little corners at the bottom upward, leaving part of closed point of the Preliminary Base showing between the small "V" shape. This makes the simple petals.

5 Turn over and repeat on other side, keeping horizontal creases at bottom level. Mountain fold (*see p. 12*) the right corner behind to shape bud. Repeat on left to finish.

6 To make calyx: start with green square in finished Waterbomb Base (*see pp. 16–17*) with closed point at bottom. Fold right flap down with crease beginning at the middle of the top edge, as shown. The flap now lies out to right of closed point.

7 Repeat Step 6 with three other flaps making the crease at slightly different angles, so that from either side all flaps are visible as shown.

8 To make the leaves: start with first green square of paper, coloured side facing upward, in a diamond shape. Fold in half diagonally from bottom to top.

9 Fold part of bottom edge up to make a thin triangular flap with crease beginning at left corner.

10 Keeping above fold, unfold square. Shape leaf by mountain folding upper and lower points and white triangular flap behind. Make four other leaves in same way. To assemble card: fold in half and arrange flower bud, calyx and leaves on front, then glue in place.

INDEX

ACKNOWLEDGMENTS

THE PUBLISHERS AND AUTHOR WOULD LIKE TO THANK THE FOLLOWING PEOPLE AND ORGANIZATIONS FOR THEIR GENEROUS HELP AND SUPPORT IN THE PRODUCTION OF THIS BOOK:

SPECIAL MESSAGE FROM THE AUTHOR
WITH ALL MY LOVE TO JULES, SIOBHAN AND GEORGINA

SPECIAL THANKS TO
THE CREATORS OF ALL ORIGAMI MODELS DETAILED.
TRADITIONAL MODELS HAVE UNKNOWN ORIGINS

CHRIS MORLEY FOR CHECKING PROOFS

KATHIE GILL FOR INDEXING

USEFUL ADDRESSES
PAPERCHASE – BRANCHES IN LONDON AND THE SOUTHEAST
(*Suppliers of of a wide range of papers*)

THE MUJI SHOP, 26 GREAT MARLBOROUGH STREET, LONDON W1V 1HL
AND 39 SHELTON STREET, LONDON WC2H 9HJ
(*Stock origami paper in 6in (15cm) square packs of 100 or
3in (7.5cm) square packs of 380 sheets*)

THE JAPAN CENTRE, 66 BREWER STREET, LONDON W1R 3PJ
(*Ornate origami paper and English and Japanese origami books
by mail order, tel: 0171–439 8035*)

BOOKS NIPPON, 64–66 ST PAULS CHURCHYARD, LONDON EC4M 8AA
(*Ornate origami paper and English and Japanese origami books
by mail order, tel: 0171–248 4956*)

WASHI UK, 6 CHAPEL LANE, BARROW-ON-TRENT, DERBY DE73 1HE
(*For a catalogue of* washi *paper send four first-class stamps
to the above address*)

ORIGAMI WORKSHOPS
RICK BEECH, THE AUTHOR, CAN BE CONTACTED IN CONNECTION WITH
WORKSHOPS OR COMMISSIONS AT 33 ORMSKIRK RISE, SPONDON,
DERBY DE21 7NU, TEL: 01332 281802

ORIGAMI SOCIETIES
BRITISH ORIGAMI SOCIETY, 35 CORFE CRESCENT HAZELGROVE,
STOCKPORT, CHESHIRE SK7 5PR

ORIGAMI USA, 15 WEST 77TH STREET, NEW YORK, NY 10024-5192, USA